Researching
Online

Researching Online

Fifth Edition

David Munger

Shireen Campbell
Davidson College

Longman

New York Boston San Francisco
London Toronto Sydney Tokyo Singapore Madrid
Mexico City Munich Paris Cape Town Hong Kong Montreal

Acquisitions Editor: Lynn Huddon
Supplements Editor: Donna Campion

Researching Online, 5/e by David Munger and Shireen Campbell

Copyright ©2002 Pearson Education, Inc. (Publishing as Longman
Publishers.)

ISBN 0-321-09277-5

1 2 3 4 5 6 7 8 9 10-DM-04 03 02 01

Contents

Preface

The process of writing this edition of *Researching Online* brings to mind a traditional story from Italy. A young tenor was performing a difficult aria in an opera house known for its demanding audiences. To his surprise, the audience's thunderous applause brought him back to the stage for encore after encore. After his fifth performance, he told the audience that he appreciated their gratitude, but his voice was failing and he could sing no more. A disgruntled voice from the back of the hall retorted, "You're going to do it until you get it right!"

With *Researching Online,* we feel fortunate to have the opportunity to try to get it right once a year. Because not only the Internet but also the level of sophistication of its users change so rapidly, a new edition each year—a rarity in the textbook industry—enables us to update, add, and adapt at a pace that *almost* approaches that of technology.

Researching Online shows students how to do research on the Internet in an easy-to-follow, step-by-step format. It's written in plain English, with clear examples of the types of materials students may encounter in their own research. The Internet is presented in the order that students will most likely encounter it: first, they learn how to get online. Then they learn about Internet resources like e-mail, real-time discussion, and the Web. Finally, they get clear, easy-to-follow instructions on creating their own Web pages.

Everything about *Researching Online* has been designed to make it the most useful possible tool for anyone doing research on the Internet. Its compact size allows it to consume little desk space in crowded computer labs. Specialized vocabulary is **bold and underlined** to alert readers to terms defined in the glossary. Text users must input is displayed in a `special typeface` to make it easy to recognize. URLs are displayed in **_bold italic_** and without confusing angle brackets. Most importantly, critical concepts are both explained in the text and reinforced visually with real-world examples.

Features in this edition

- A revised opening chapter that argues that the Internet remains the most powerful research tool on the planet, despite recent well-publicized failures in the commercial sector
- A revised search engine chapter that now focuses on Google and the Open Directory Project, while cautioning students that third-generation sites like Google (and now many of the "old standards" such as AltaVista) rank search results by popularity—not necessarily an indicator of accuracy or reliability
- An expanded Tips feature that covers issues of both electronic etiquette and ethics and responsible computer use
- An additional chapter, which covers an extended sample research project on a medical research topic
- A completely revised chapter on creating Web sites now emphasizes creating simple sites using Microsoft Word
- Additions to the newsgroup chapter cover Web-based discussion as well as the new Web news searching tool at **_http://groups.google.com/_**
- Updated examples and URLs throughout the text

Acknowledgments

This book evolved out of the groundbreaking book _Teaching Online_ by Daniel Anderson, Bret Benjamin, Christopher Busiel, and Bill Paredes-Holt. Jeremy Campbell provided great advice, and Jonathan Campbell provided great inspiration, as always. Jimmy and Nora Munger continue to demonstrate how easy it can be to use and learn from computers. Lynn Huddon and Donna Campion at Longman were rock-solid in their support of this book. Chrysta Meadowbrooke provided brilliant copyediting. Finally, our gratitude goes to this text's reviewers, Bonny Bryan, Santa Barbara City College; Stephen M. Byars, University of Southern California; Patrick J. Hurley, Saint Louis University; Mary Hurst, Cuyahoga Community College, Western Campus; and Eric Loring, Scottsdale Community College.

Chapter 1

The Internet Step by Step

The Internet as research tool

You know the Internet can be used to shop, book travel reservations, read movie reviews, and get definitions of unfamiliar words quickly. But in the past year, the Internet has been rocked with bad news. Viruses have been created and circulated, sometimes harming personal computers or bringing business to a temporary halt. Some prominent Internet companies have gone under, while others have lost important court battles. With constant stories in the news such as "Dot Com Bubble Bursts," "Chat Room Blamed for Child's Disappearance," and "Another Internet Start-up Fails," you may wonder if you can or should count on the Internet for assistance with your classes. The short answer is yes, and the long answer is the subject of *Researching Online*.

The Internet was developed to facilitate research, and it remains the most powerful research tool today. The same features that make the Internet easy to use for buying CDs also make it a tremendous tool for college researchers. For example:

- You are giving a report on Toni Morrison in Contemporary American Fiction in six and a half hours and want to double-check the year in which she won the Pulitzer Prize, but at 2:00 A.M., the university library is closed and your mom is in bed.

1

- Your Psychology 101 class requires you to participate in one experiment as part of the subject pool. To decide which one you want to be part of, you need to read the experiment descriptions and then sign up for the one that interests you most.
- Studying abroad in Italy, you have time to visit only the Uffizi Gallery or the Galleria dell'Accademia in the next week and need to ask your former Art History professor which one you should go to.
- You are working on a Chemistry lab report, and you need to know the boiling point of nitrogen dioxide.
- You're not sure about the reliability of a source you want to use in an oral presentation about the most recent explosion of violence in the Middle East, but it's too new to have published reviews.

Can the Internet answer all of your research questions? Well, it doesn't contain the entire archives of the Library of Congress or even every back issue of the *New York Times* (not yet, anyway). It can't perform original research experiments or help you communicate with someone who doesn't have Internet access. And while it can help you reach people and resources on the other side of the world, it's certainly no substitute for live, one-on-one interaction with real people and real things.

The Internet is at its best when it helps make your research experience easier, more thorough, and more collaborative. At other times, you may need to rely on the permanence and authority of resources found in traditional libraries. This book will help guide you through the process of integrating online sources into your research.

Connecting to the Internet

Connecting via the campus network

Most colleges and universities have a network of computers that is connected to the Internet. In many cases, computers are available for student use in computer labs, the library, or in dorms. The software you need to access the Internet has been installed; all you need to do is learn to use the software on those computers, and you're in business (see Chapters 2–6). For e-mail, you'll need to establish an e-mail account—usually handled through your campus computer services department.

Connecting using your own computer

If you have your own computer, getting connected to the Internet is a little more complicated—but once you're connected, it's a lot more convenient than relying on public computers. If you have a brand-new computer, all the software you need is already installed on your computer. If you have inherited an older computer, especially one that has never been connected to the Internet, you may have to do a bit of scrambling to obtain the software you need. If you need to subscribe to an Internet service provider for Internet access (see below), the software is often provided as part of your subscription cost. Your campus computer services or information technology department may also offer free Internet access software.

Direct access. Many institutions offer direct access to the Internet in campus dorms. If you live on campus and your campus offers this service, it's worth it to buy any equipment you need to connect directly—the connection will be much faster and more reliable than any other means of Internet connection. Usually all you'll need is an Ethernet card and a login name and password. Before you buy anything, double-check with your campus computer services department to see what equipment you need.

Remote access. If you don't live on campus, or if your dorm isn't wired for direct access, then you probably need to connect via a commercial **Internet service provider** (ISP). Some colleges have made arrangements with Internet service providers to provide free or low-cost access for off-campus students, but most students are on their own when it comes to Internet access. There are now several different types of Internet service available, but these services will typically offer a flat monthly rate for unlimited Internet access. Depending on your budget and what's available in your area, you may choose **cable modem**, **direct subscriber line** (DSL), **satellite**, or **dial-up** access. To help determine which of these services is right for you, consult Table 1.1.

How the Internet works

Once you're connected, you can begin to explore the Internet. The Internet is a worldwide network of computers that are connected to each other in many different ways. Each of these different sorts of connections is useful for dif-

Service	Speed/Cost	Requirements/ Contact info
Cable modem	256–2000 kbps $40–70/month $100–300 for equipment/ installation	Ethernet card, cable modem. Your building must be wired for cable. You may be required to purchase cable TV. *http://www.rr.com/ or contact your local cable company.*
Direct subscriber line (DSL)	256–1024 kbps $50–100/month $100 for installation	Ethernet card, DSL modem. You must live within 1–2 miles of a tele-phone office. *Contact your local phone company.*
Satellite	56–400 kbps $30–50/month $200–300 for equipment/ installation	Windows computer, satellite dish, satellite modem, Ethernet card, modem, phone line. *http://www.direcpc.com/*
Dial-up	56 kbps $10–30/month	Modem, phone line. *http://www.earthlink.net/, http://download.att.net/ partners/*

Table 1.1: Internet access options. With Internet access, you generally get what you pay for. Speed is measured in **kbps**—the bigger this number, the faster your connection.

ferent kinds of work. The most important Internet services are listed below.

World Wide Web. Now the most important part of the Internet, the Web allows you to quickly and easily navigate through millions of hypertext sites containing images, text, sound, motion pictures, and even databases.

E-mail. E-mail allows you to quickly exchange messages and computer files with anyone connected to the Internet.

Real-time discussion. A variety of programs allow you to chat almost instantly with other users.

Usenet newsgroups. Newsgroups are a vast collection of specialized electronic bulletin boards where (usually) anyone can post or respond to a message.

Listservs. A specialized type of e-mail, listservs are moderated or unmoderated discussion groups on specified topics.

Telnet, FTP, and **Gopher.** Older parts of the Internet, these are ways of accessing files and programs on distant computers.

For more on how the Internet works, visit Learn the Net at *http://www.learnthenet.com.*

URLs: Addresses on the Internet

The Internet has no center. There is no single computer or group of computers in the "middle" of the Internet. There isn't even a "map" or physical representation of how all the computers on the Internet are connected. The only thing everyone on the Internet has agreed upon is how resources are named. Every resource on the Internet has a unique name, different from every other resource on the Internet. Once you know a resource's name, you don't need to know where it is, what kind of computer it's on, or how to get there. All the information you need to find every resource on the Internet is included in the name itself.

Names on the Internet are called **URLs** (**Uniform Resource Locators**). A URL has several parts:

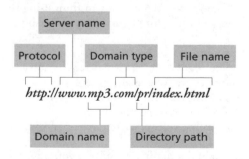

The **protocol** indicates the type of link to be made with the server. In this case, it's *http:*, which stands for *hypertext transfer protocol*—the protocol used for all resources on the

World Wide Web. The **domain** name is registered by the Web site owner, in this case, the mp3.com Corporation. The **server name** (usually *www* for Web sites) refers to the server the site owner uses to host the Web site. The **domain type** indicates what type of organization the owner is, here a commercial organization. The **directory path** reflects the overall organization of the Web site. This resource is located in the *pr* **directory**. The **file name** is the name the site owner has given to the particular resource you're looking at, here a listing of mp3.com press releases. Note that slashes are used to separate directory names from each other and from the domain name and file name. Two slashes are used to separate the protocol from the domain name.

When you pronounce a URL, you can save time by using a few common conventions. If the person you're speaking to knows you're referring to a Web address, you can leave out the *http://*. Then say, "www dot mp3 dot com slash pr slash index dot html." Make sure you spell out any words with unconventional spellings (in most cases, you can leave out the *index.html* or *index.htm,* too). However, when you refer to URLs in formal research, always give the complete URL.

Use the Internet to inform your research

In one sense, the Internet is an enormous, constantly evolving conversation in which users meet to discuss almost any imaginable topic. You can benefit from using the Internet in dozens of ways; for instance, you can easily:

- Access online resources to support your research, including many resources like databases and live "cams" that aren't available in any other format.
- Communicate with authors of important sources or experts in various fields of study.
- Meet online with other researchers to discuss a common topic.
- Design and publish the results of your research on the World Wide Web, offering an interactive Web site, links to other Internet resources about the topic, video clips of major figures, and forums for conversation among users.

Online versus printed sources

Online sources and printed sources each have strengths and weaknesses. Therefore, deciding when to use which type of source isn't a matter of applying a simple formula. To determine what type of resource will be most valuable for your research project, you'll first need to consider how you are planning to use the source. Table 1.2 summarizes the most important differences between online and printed sources, but remember that there are many different types of printed and online sources—these guidelines don't necessarily apply to all cases.

Suppose you are researching endangered loggerhead sea turtles on the Florida coast. For authoritative information about the physiology and behavior of sea turtles, books and journal articles will probably offer the most reliable information. But the Internet is the only place you'll find a real-

Online Resources	Printed Resources
Can be easily modified	Unchangeable except in a new edition
Can include many different media	Only include text and images
May appear different to different users	Appear the same to each user
Allow input from users	Do not allow user input
Inexpensive to produce	Relatively expensive to produce
Allow almost anyone to publish information	Publishing closely monitored by "gatekeepers" such as editors and librarians
Generally not subjected to scholarly review	Often reviewed by scholars for accuracy and relevance

Table 1.2: Comparison of online resources and printed resources

time map of the movements of sea turtles as they are electronically tracked by researchers.

The Internet and print sources can offer different types of information, but they can also offer the same information. For example, you can find the text of thousands of classic works of literature such as James Fenimore Cooper's *The Last of the Mohicans* on the World Wide Web, and you can also find many of the same works in your school library. How do you decide which source to use in your research? The answer depends on

- how you'll be using the information (for what kind of project, for example)
- the degree to which the versions are identical and equally accurate

Select sources based on the demands of your project

Each project has different demands. A thesis paper on Cooper may require that you find the most authoritative edition of *The Last of the Mohicans* available. A two-page outline for an in-class presentation on descriptions and uses of specific weapons in *The Last of the Mohicans* may require a searchable version of the text, such as those available online. Here is a list of issues to consider as you determine which sources will be most useful for your project.

1. **Course requirements.** Your instructor may require that all (or a certain number) of your research sources be from academic books or refereed journal articles. In this case, though you may want to use an online service to locate resources, you will most likely find the actual resources in a library. On the other hand, if your instructor requires that you interview an expert in a field, you may be more likely to make that contact via the Internet.

2. **Accessibility.** If everyone had access to a library with thousands of journal subscriptions and millions of volumes, traditional sources might often be the best option. However, most of us don't have that luxury, so online sources become a more important component of the research process.

3. **Timeliness.** In many cases, particularly with newsgroups and listservs, the Internet can provide more up-to-date information than traditional sources. And while daily newspapers offer a reliable, traditional re-

search source, most major newspapers are now available on the World Wide Web, with searchable indexes of past issues.

4. **Authority.** Printed resources, especially those available in a college library, are often reviewed by scholars for accuracy and relevance—if this sort of authority is required for your project, refereed journals and academic books will probably be your most important sources. In other cases, an Internet source may carry more authority than the resources available in the library. For example, you may find a facsimile edition of a classic work of literature on the Web.

5. **Reliability.** Pay close attention to the matters discussed in the following section, "Evaluate all sources you use." As you locate both printed and online sources in your research, evaluate them according to the criteria outlined below. When you have a choice, select the most reliable sources, whether online or in print.

Evaluate all sources you use

One of the most important virtues of the Internet is its universality. For about a hundred dollars, anyone can register a World Wide Web address and have as much of a Web presence as Microsoft or Amazon.com. The Internet has no gatekeeper (for that matter, it has no single, central gate).

While the Internet's universality is positive because it allows previously marginalized voices to be heard, it also adds a new layer of difficulty for researchers. The gatekeepers of traditional research sources—editors, academics, and librarians—work hard to ensure that any source in a college library meets a basic standard of reliability and authenticity.

Since the Internet lacks those gatekeepers, you're just as likely to encounter the rantings of one unqualified individual there as you are to find a resource that's unavailable in any other form. Some sites may seem totally legitimate, but the authors' careless incorporation of information from other sources amounts to plagiarism. Using such a site as one of your sources only compounds the error. You will also want to study what group or institution is sponsoring the site and consider what possible biases that sponsorship may imply.

Additionally, materials found online often differ considerably from those in print. Internet resources may feature graphics, sound, and video, for example. They may have a more (or less) impressive appearance than traditional "published" articles. And what about instances in which you can find both print copies of articles in your library or through interlibrary loan and online versions through sources such as Lexis Nexis? In some cases, the online versions may be abbreviated, lacking relevant tables, graphs, and charts—or even the author's credentials.

When you're evaluating an electronic source, above all, you must ask questions, and never assume the source is an authority. Only sources that are relevant to your project (see Table 1.3 and the tips given above), that are reliable, and that include authentic, accurate information should be used in research projects.

Finally, always ask yourself: what is the relative value of the Web site in comparison to the range of other information resources available on this topic? Check with a librarian to ensure that you have explored the other resources (print and nonprint) available in this area. Never let the ease of using the Internet replace altogether a visit to your library.

Figure 1.1 shows an example of a Web site that provides many answers to the questions presented in Table 1.3. The site is well designed, gives information about the author's credentials, and is regularly updated. Note that the ads and awards on the site don't necessarily add or remove from the site's value, but they should be investigated in case they reveal a bias or hidden agenda. Before you use an electronic source in your research, make sure you find answers to the questions in this section.

Writing instructors and librarians recognize the difficulty in evaluating electronic sources, and some have attempted to generate uniform criteria for evaluating these sources. You may want to check out the Using Cyber-sources Web site at *http://www.devry-phx.edu/lrnresrc/dowsc/integrty.htm* for a detailed set of guidelines on how to evaluate a Web source, as well as links to other sites with more suggestions. Another site, *http://www.namss.org.uk/evaluate.htm,* includes links to a wide range of resources to help you in selecting only the best sources for your research. You can also check out possible sites with a tool, such as the Argus Clearinghouse, that rates and reviews sites and lists them according to topic (*http://www.clearinghouse.net*).

Most guides for evaluating online sources are focused primarily on Web sites, but you can use many of the same strategies for evaluating other online sources, such as newsgroups, real-time discussions, or multimedia presentations. Because of the anonymity the Internet confers, online dis-

Aspect	Questions
Author/ Purpose	Who is the author?
	Is a link to the author's *home page* (see page 67) and/or e-mail contact information provided?
	Does the author have an academic or professional affiliation?
	Who is the sponsor of the resource? An academic organization? A business?
	What are the potential biases/hidden agendas of the author/sponsor of the resource?
	Who is the intended audience for this site?
	What is the site's purpose—to inform? to argue for a position? to solicit business or support?
Content	How comprehensive is this site?
	Is the resource regularly updated?
	Is the information that is presented accurate?
	How are sources documented?
	On what basis are *links* (see p. 35) selected? Are the links provided up-to-date?
	Are the articles reviewed by peers? (Note: Beware of "Top 500 Web site" awards and the like—always check *them* out using the standards given here. Some Web sites are even devoted to giving out phony awards—for a hilarious example, check out *http://www.thecorporation.com/icon/icon.html.*)
Design	Is the site easy to navigate and use?
	Does the resource follow good principles of design and proper grammar and style? (Note: Good design is not necessarily flashy. A simple site can be more tasteful than one bristling with graphics and sound effects.)

Table 1.3: Questions to ask when evaluating an online source

Figure 1.1: What to look for when evaluating a Web site

cussions are particularly difficult to evaluate. It's impossible to be sure who you're conversing with, and therefore it's nearly impossible to assess the reliability of such a source. However, online discussions are a great place to get ideas for research—as long as you can independently verify the ideas through a more reliable source.

Record all citation information for documentation purposes

As you research, be sure to record all information about the sources you find interesting. Before you do so, check with your instructor to verify which format for documentation your class will be using and record all information in that format from the beginning.

TIP

Ethics and etiquette. Throughout this book, look for our brief tips on research ethics and etiquette to help you conduct research ethically and present a polished image on the Net.

Chapter 2

E-Mail

E-mail is the "killer app" of the Internet. Without e-mail, the Net might be no more influential than a new television channel. E-mail transforms the Internet into a communications tool with the power of a billion minds, all connected by a simple system of addresses. E-mail is much more than a way to keep in touch with friends—it is a collaboration and organizational tool that, if it hasn't already, will likely become the "home office" of your busy life.

E-mail is most effective when you think of creative ways to make it even more useful. You can e-mail yourself reminders of important events or deadlines. You can e-mail groups of people with a single click to announce events or just stay in touch. You can subscribe to automated services that notify you of anything from the date of your favorite television show to your parents' wedding anniversary.

Using e-mail in your research

You can use e-mail in any of the following ways:

- To connect with members of the class on an individual basis and with the instructor outside of class and office hours
- To send inquiries to the instructor, for example, if you have missed class or have a question about an assignment
- To turn in papers or other homework
- To obtain resources for a research project, from **list-servs** (see page 22), the **World Wide Web** (see Chap-

ter 4), other students, or your instructor
- To conduct online "interviews" or surveys to gather data for your research

E-mail is also an invaluable tool for collaborating with others:

- You can e-mail drafts and comments to peer-review partners with the advantage of being able to ask questions and carry on a dialogue.
- When working on collective projects, you can use e-mail to brainstorm about ideas, share work, or coordinate meeting times.
- You can e-mail resources and materials that you have found to students who have similar research topics.

How e-mail works

To send and receive e-mail, you need an e-mail program. Usually this software is already installed on your computer: the major World Wide Web **browsers**, Netscape Communicator and Microsoft Internet Explorer, include e-mail programs—Messenger and Outlook Express, respectively. It is also easy to find many other e-mail programs with different features and characteristics. For instance, you could visit *http://www.eudora.com* and download Eudora, a free e-mail-only program favored by many Internet veterans.

You send and receive messages through a **mail server**, a program on a computer connected to the Internet which organizes, stores, and distributes e-mail messages to various users. Servers exchange with each other (often through a chain of several servers in different locations across the country or worldwide) using two-part e-mail **addresses**.

Addresses and their elements

A typical e-mail address contains two elements. The **mailbox name** or **user's name** appears before the @ sign (pronounced "at"), and the **domain** information, representing the server that provides e-mail to the user, follows the @ sign. A sample message might use these addresses:

```
From: dave@wordmunger.com
To: shcampbell@davidson.edu
```

The mailbox name of the sender is *dave*. The recipient's mailbox name is *shcampbell*.

The domain generally contains information about the organization and organization type. Elements of the domain are separated by a period (.) generally called a *dot*. Here, the sender's domain includes the name of the organization, *wordmunger*, and an abbreviation describing the type of organization, *com* (commercial site). The mailbox of the recipient, *shcampbell*, is registered with the organization *davidson*, classified as *edu* (educational institution).

In the United States, the standard domain types are:

```
.edu = educational institution
.com = commercial organization
.gov = government organization
.mil = military institution
.org = (often) nonprofit organization
.net = (often) Internet service provider
.biz = business
.info = information site (usually business)
```

Outside the United States, domain names usually end in a two-letter element indicating the country of origin: for example, *.jp* (Japan), *.nl* (the Netherlands), and *.eg* (Egypt).

Many e-mail programs allow you to save addresses in a file called an *address book,* which makes it unnecessary to retype an address. You can even assign more than one address to each entry (often called a **nickname** or **group**) in your address book, so you can send e-mail to many people simply by typing one entry in your e-mail message. For example, if you are working on a group project in English 101, you could create the address book entry "Eng_101_group" to instantly send a message to everyone in your group.

Getting connected

We recommend that all students set up an e-mail account. Most colleges and universities have already incorporated computer and Internet fees into tuition costs, so they generally offer "free" or very inexpensive e-mail accounts to students and faculty. Although some students will inevitably have problems along the way, setting up an account is usually a fairly simple process. For more information on Internet connection, see pages 2–3.

Setting up an e-mail account may take a little time, so request your account very early in the term. Learn about your systems by reading any handouts with detailed step-by-step instructions. Since schools frequently change e-mail procedures from term to term as they expand their computer services, bear in mind that some of the instructions may be incorrect. To verify that your account is working, send yourself a test message.

Using your e-mail program

Most people send and receive e-mail messages using an e-mail program on a personal computer. The e-mail program can talk to mail servers, which are programs on Internet-connected machines that store and distribute electronic messages.

E-mail programs (Microsoft Outlook Express is probably the most popular) allow you to both compose messages to send to others and retrieve mail from the mail server and bring it to your machine. You can even send and receive files (**attachments**) you created using another program such as Microsoft Word or Adobe Photoshop.

In Outlook Express (Figure 2.1), by clicking on items across the top bar, you can save a draft of your message and control whether or not to use your **signature file** (which

Figure 2.1: An e-mail message composed in Outlook Express

TIP

E-mail viruses. Everyone has heard of <u>viruses</u>, the pernicious programs that can cripple or disable a computer. Viruses are often spread through e-mail attachments. You should never open an attachment file—even one sent by someone you know—unless you know what's in the file. Be particularly careful with file names ending in `.exe` or `.bat`, because these files are programs that will begin their work as soon as you open them.

Outlook saves for you in another window—see page 26). The Send Now button mails this message, and the Send Later button prepares the message; the outgoing message will not be sent until you select a menu command to send and receive messages. This feature is useful if you want to minimize the time you are actually connected to the Internet (if a modem and a phone share the same line, or if you are using a laptop while it is not connected to the Internet).

Before you can use it to send and receive messages, you need to tell your e-mail program how to access your account. In Outlook Express, your account information is kept in the Accounts panel. Other programs may keep this information in the Preferences panel. Your campus computer services department or Internet service provider should give you the correct information to input when you register your account. Here is an example of an Account panel that has been configured to send and receive mail.

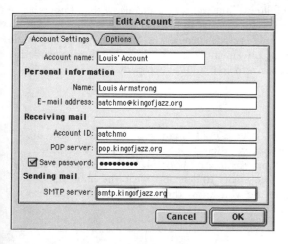

Once you set up the information, you will never have to retype your e-mail address, your signature file, or other information. Of course, you will always have access to the configurations, so you can modify the program's settings to your liking.

E-mail conventions

By its nature, e-mail tends to be less formal than regular mail ("snail mail"). Some have suggested that e-mail compares more closely with spoken conversation than formal letter writing. That's probably a good thing, because it allows people to concentrate on getting their message across quickly instead of focusing on decorum. However, you should still take care when composing a message because, unlike spoken conversation, an e-mail message cannot convey the subtle nuances of speech such as intonation and facial expression.

You should also be aware that your recipient's e-mail program may not display text formatting (such as **bold** and *italic*) in the same way as your e-mail program. It's probably best to use the _underscore_ character to represent italic text and *asterisks* for emphasis.

A debate is currently raging about whether messages should contain unedited typographical errors and abbreviations like *BTW* ("by the way"), *FWIW* ("for what it's worth"), *IMHO* ("in my humble opinion"), *msg* ("message"), *mtg* ("meeting"), and *shd* ("should"). One side of the argument suggests that the immediacy of e-mail is diminished when writers must take time to follow all the rigors of academic writing. Others argue that the development of an Internet "code" of communication unnecessarily excludes people who aren't "in the know" while offering a convenient excuse for those who haven't made the effort to learn to communicate properly.

TIP

ETIQUETTE: **E-mail language.** When in doubt, use conservative language in your e-mail messages. Don't use shortcuts like *BTW* or *IMHO* unless you're sure your recipients understand what the abbreviations mean and you know them well enough to address them by their first names.

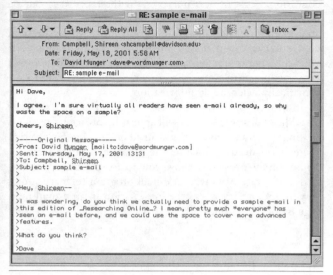

Figure 2.2: An example of an e-mail with a reply quotation

Another e-mail convention arose because of the ease with which computer technology reproduces text. When you **reply** to an e-mail message, you can usually include the original message in the response (see Figure 2.2 for an example). The text that is quoted from the original message is denoted with an **angle bracket** (>) before each line of text. Most e-mail programs automatically quote the whole text of the preceding message into the reply, so reply quotations can get quite long with little or no effort of your own. A good rule of thumb is to include a reply quotation only for important

--- TIP ---

ETIQUETTE: E-mail reply quotations. An unnecessarily long reply quotation can be an annoyance to your recipient. To save space and time, delete the portions of a reply quotation that are no longer relevant.

ETHICS: Remember to protect the privacy of your correspondents. Don't send someone else's e-mail message to another person without the author's permission. When working in a group, it's a good idea to agree in advance that everyone in the group can freely forward work to the others.

educational or business purposes. In these cases, it can be useful to "overhear" part of the original conversation or to analyze the original message a second time. Make sure you contextualize the material you quote in your response. If your message is not mission-critical, it's easy to delete text that's no longer relevant, or to set your e-mail program to automatically delete reply information.

In most e-mail programs, each time you quote a message an additional angle bracket will appear before each line. This nesting of quotations continues until one reader decides that there is no need to include the older text, and deletes it. Some e-mail programs allow you to format quotes differently. Be aware of how your e-mail program formats quotes so you understand where the information in an e-mail message is coming from.

What is a listserv?

A *listserv,* also known as a *mailing list, list,* or *group,* is a program that allows e-mail to be sent to a group of addresses simultaneously. (Throughout this text we will use the term *listserv* generically to denote a range of mailing list programs including Listserv, Majordomo, Listproc, and Web-based mailing lists.) Though listservs vary according to function, type, and administration, each listserv defines a narrow subject area which all posts are expected to fall within. For example, the discussion list *MODBRITS* carefully defines its scope as "Modern British and Irish Literature: 1895–1955," and participants are expected to abide by the list's geographic and chronological limits.

Make sure you follow a listserv discussion for a period of time to clarify the nature of the listserv's audience and learn what constitutes an interesting or convincing message on that list. Sometimes the boundaries of allowable topics on a list are very narrowly defined. For example, the *h-latam* list (a discussion of Latin American history) defines its subject to exclude current events in Latin America. Because the list sees its function as providing a level-headed discussion of "historical" events, potentially heated political discussions of more recent events in Latin America are discouraged. A post discussing causes and effects of the Zapatista uprising in Chiapas, Mexico, for instance, would not be allowed on the list unless it was directed solely to bibliographic source material or pedagogical concerns.

TIP

ETHICS: **Listserv messages.** Don't send a message to a list just to pass the time or to try to sell a car (unless the list is for the purpose of selling used cars). For most lists, posts like this would be frowned upon and might result in a number of angry messages (or **flames**) from list members. Some lists have **moderators** who screen messages before sending them to the full list in order to ensure their relevance. Repeated inflammatory or "off-topic" messages from a user can result in removal from the list. Remember that your message is going to a large audience. Ask yourself if your message is likely to be useful to all the members of the list. Also remember that your issue may have been discussed before you became a member of the list.

For gathering substantive research material, the most useful lists are those posting items like news stories, articles, documents, and expert commentary. However, you should not give up on a list simply because it focuses on discussion, for you can learn a lot by keeping track of and participating in active listserv debates. You will see how opinions are formed, revised, and complicated, and how multiple perspectives can inform a topic.

Using listservs to facilitate research conversations

Your instructor may create class listservs or nicknames to make announcements, revise reading or meeting schedules, forward supplementary material, start discussion, or ask for feedback on a particular topic. Lists and nicknames also give you the opportunity to contribute material for course reading and to share relevant resources with the entire class.

How to subscribe to a listserv

Finding listservs on your research topic

The easiest way to find a listserv is to do a search on the World Wide Web (see Chapter 4 for more information on browsing the Web). Point your browser to a mailing list **search engine** like *http://www.list-universe.com/* or *http://tile.net/lists/*. There, you can search using **keywords** appropriate to your topic or browse through directories of mailing lists that may be of interest to you. For more on keyword searching, see pp. 41–47.

If you're not sure about a listserv, just subscribe to it for a few days to see if it's useful. If it's not useful to you, you can easily unsubscribe.

Subscribing to a listserv is complicated by the fact that there are three major types of listservs: **Listserv**, **Listproc**, and **Majordomo**, in addition to the newer Web-based lists discussed on page 25. Fortunately, it's easy to distinguish between the three types because the address you e-mail to subscribe always begins with *listserv, listproc,* or *majordomo.* Never type anything in the subject line, regardless of the type of list you're subscribing to.

Listserv. To subscribe to this type of list, send e-mail to the administrative address for the list you want to subscribe to. For example, if you want to subscribe to the African American Women's Literature list, you send the following e-mail message:

```
To: listserv@cmuvm.csv.cmich.edu
subscribe AAWOMLIT your name
```

Don't literally type "your name," unless that's what it says on your birth certificate. If your name is Fred Jones, type that in place of *your name*. The convention in this book is to indicate where you need to fill in your own information by using *italic* type. By the way, one of the most common mistakes beginning computer users make is to literally type in everything they see in the documentation. Whenever you're learning a new program, take a moment to see if the documentation has a special way of indicating information you need to provide yourself—usually, you'll find the going much easier.

Listproc. Subscribing to a Listproc list works the same way as a Listserv list. For example, to subscribe to the Listproc American Literature, send the following e-mail:

```
To: listproc@lists.missouri.edu
subscribe AMLIT-L your name
```

Majordomo. Since Majordomo servers aren't as sophisticated as Listserv or Listproc, you usually need to include your e-mail address in the subscribe message. For example, to subscribe to the Postcolonial list, send the following e-mail:

```
To: majordomo@jefferson.village.virginia.edu
subscribe postcolonial your e-mail address
```

Unsubscribing from a listserv

To unsubscribe from the lists above, send the following messages:

Listserv
```
To: listserv@cmuvm.csv.cmich.edu
signoff AAWOMLIT
```

Listproc
```
To: listproc@lists.missouri.edu
signoff AMLIT-L
```

Majordomo
```
To: majordomo@jefferson.village.virginia.edu
unsubscribe postcolonial your e-mail address
```

Web-based lists

Several services now allow anyone to create an e-mail list using only a Web browser. Here are three of the most popular:

Yahoo! Groups
http://groups.yahoo.com/

Listbot
http://www.listbot.com/

Topica
http://www.topica.com/

Lists hosted by these services may not be listed in mailing list search engines. To find a Web-based list, generally you'll need to visit the host site (for example, *http://groups.yahoo.com*) and use the service's proprietary search function. You could also use one of these services to create your own group e-mail list. Note: Because Web-based lists are so easy to create, they may not be as academically rigorous as traditional listservs. In addition, many Web sites now offer their own mailing lists which you subscribe to by following the directions on the site.

Emoticons and other e-mail miscellany

Many Internet users attempt to express sarcasm and light-hearted emotion by using **emoticons** (usually called **smileys**). Smileys are roughly the Internet equivalent of a wink, and about as sophisticated. Though they often denote a lack of careful writing, smileys sometimes help clarify the author's intention. The basic smiley is a sideways happy face :-) (tilt your head to the left to read it), although a host of others can be used to express a broad range of emotions (see Table 2.1). Though a writer might incorporate a smiley in informal prose, it would be preferable in a formal composition to use words to convey irony effectively. Remember, if you say something truly offensive, adding a smiley after it isn't going to do a lot to cool down the offended party.

Another way to personalize e-mail communication is by adding a *signature* or *sig file.* A signature is a section of text automatically appended to the bottom of an e-mail message. Signatures are a way to identify the author and place him or her socially and professionally. Besides supplying the writer's e-mail address to facilitate replies, a signature often carries a writer's professional or academic affiliations, physical address and other contact information, or a favorite quotation. Many e-mail programs allow you to create several different signatures: for example, one for personal correspondance and one for use in formal research.

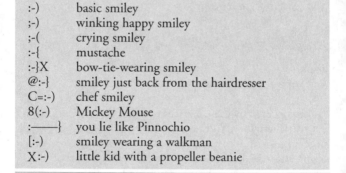

:-)	basic smiley
;-)	winking happy smiley
;-(	crying smiley
:-{	mustache
:-}X	bow-tie-wearing smiley
@:-}	smiley just back from the hairdresser
C=:-)	chef smiley
8(:-)	Mickey Mouse
:——}	you lie like Pinnochio
[:-)	smiley wearing a walkman
X:-)	little kid with a propeller beanie

Table 2.1: A small sampling of smileys
Taken from *ftp://ftp.wwa.com/pub/Scarecrow/Misc/Smilies*

Chapter 3

Real-Time Discussion

Explore the range of real-time discussions

When the Internet was first being created, its developers realized that it had tremendous potential as a communications device. Some of the earliest applications enabled users to communicate directly to each other, in "real time," rather than sending a delayed message like an e-mail message. What makes **real-time discussion** interesting is that multiple users around the globe can communicate in real time with only a slight lag between exchanges.

These areas of the Internet are still widely used today, but Web programmers have now enabled these same features through the more intuitive Web interface. You may have shared pictures with friends or kept up with your family through a popular program like AOL's Instant Messenger, or you may have visited a **chat room** at a Web site you frequent. Each Web-based chat room has its own features and limitations, but this chapter will show you how to use **ichat**, one of the most common interfaces, which is included free with many Addison Wesley Longman textbooks. Your classes may also use a course management program such as Blackboard or Web CT, so these resources are discussed briefly below.

The almost instantaneous transfer of messages in real-time discussion allows users to communicate in a way that resembles face-to-face conversation. Unlike e-mail or newsgroups, which are **asynchronous** (i.e., there is an expected delay between messages), real-time discussion allows for synchronous conversation.

This immediacy can present a problem: if your audience is not physically present, how can you convey the sorts of nonverbal signals (expressions, gestures, tone of voice, etc.) that people use in conversation? Internet developers have come up with an answer: users can send signals that indicate an action other than speech. In ichat, users can define emotions (**emotes**) and then transmit them to other users with a click of a mouse. In this way users can interact through writing—not only with conversational dialogue but also by describing that dialogue.

A helpful way to look at real-time discussions is as a hybrid that blends elements of writing and speech. A discussion in this medium reads a little like a manuscript of a play, in which a scrolling screen displays participants' names followed by their dialogue or emotes. This sense of the theatrical is compounded by the fact that users are often referred to as characters, and they often take on pseudonyms while online.

Participate in your class chat room

Many Longman textbooks have a companion Web site that features an online chat room. If you use one of these texts, then your class can use the chat room on Longman's Web site. For example, the companion site for John Lannon's *Technical Communication,* eighth edition, is at *http://www.awlonline.com/lannontech.* To access the chat room for *Technical Communication*, you click on the collaborative network link, and then click on ichat in the left-hand column of the page (see Figure 3.1). You'll be asked to enter a nickname (usually just your first name—this is the name that will identify you to other users in your chat session), select a chat type, and click on Enter Chat Area to enter. Select i-Chat plugin (Netscape) to use the ichat plug-in; if you don't already have this plug-in, then your computer should automatically download it (see Chapter 5 for more on downloading helper applications). If you don't want to download the plug-in, select one of the other options, depending on your browser software. The ichat plug-in should offer the best performance for most users.

Once you've logged on to ichat, you need to enter a room with the other discussants for your book. Click on the Show

Map icon in the ichat toolbar. A list of textbooks should appear in the upper-right corner of your browser window. You can scroll down until you locate your textbook title, or use the "find" command in your browser to quickly locate it. Click on the book title, and you're in a discussion room for users of your book. You can use this room to conduct your discussion, or create a private room limited to class mem-

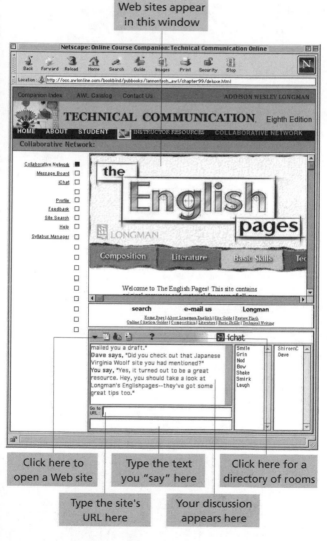

Web sites appear
in this window

Click here to
open a Web site

Type the text
you "say" here

Click here for a
directory of rooms

Type the site's
URL here

Your discussion
appears here

Figure 3.1: An ichat session

Chapter 4

The World Wide Web

Using the World Wide Web in your research

When you begin a research project, start by thinking about the ways in which the Web might be able to help. For example, if you are writing a paper on the importance of World War I in Virginia Woolf's *Mrs. Dalloway,* you can search the Web for online commentary on this issue. You can locate experts who may be able to help you find other resources on the subject. You can even use the Web to locate printed resources in your school library, as well as other resources that may be available via interlibrary loan.

If you are creating a Web page on pollution in the Ganges River in India, you can look for updates on the problem from global environmental agencies. You can find reports on the issue from online news services. You can locate other Web sites devoted to the same issue or related issues. You can request copies of journal articles on the subject to be faxed directly to you.

Even though the Web is vastly different from traditional research sources, you can still follow the same steps when using the Web as a research tool as when you use a traditional library. You still need to narrow your topic, refine searches, and evaluate source materials. Here's a summary of how the Web can be used with the steps in a traditional research project.

- **Finding a topic.** Surf the Web or perform keyword searches (see below) as you brainstorm on possible topics.

Back button takes you to the previous page visited

The URL of the current page

Paid advertisement

Clicking on side-bar expands it into a list of fa-vorites, recently visited sites, etc.

Pointer changes into hand when it moves over hot text

Use scroll bars to see the rest of the document

Figure 4.1: A sample page on the World Wide Web

Favorites command (Note: This book gives only Explorer commands; see Table 4.1 for the Navigator equivalent). Favorites allow you to save the URLs of sites you've found to be particularly useful so you can easily find them later. You can even organize your favorites into folders according to different research topics. If you do forget to save one of your sources as a favorite, you can often find it using the **History**

command. Clicking on the History tab on the sidebar in Explorer (or selecting History from the Window menu) will show you a list of the sites you have visited recently. Just click on the site's URL to return to that page, then add it to your favorites list by selecting Add Page to Favorites from the Favorites menu.

Searching the Web

When you use a browser for the first time, you almost invariably will be pointed to a **search engine** or **subject directory**. These are simply Web sites that allow you to search for the particular resources you're looking for on the World Wide Web. With a search engine, you can type a word or set of words, and

---

TIP

ETIQUETTE: Using favorites on public computers. When you're using a public computer, save your favorites to a diskette so the computer's Favorites menu doesn't get cluttered by dozens of users' personal favorites, and so you can use them on a different computer. In Explorer, you save favorites by first choosing Favorites from the Window menu, then choosing Export Favorites from the File menu.

Explorer Term	Navigator Equivalent
Address	Location
Favorites	Bookmarks
Export Favorites	Save as
Import Favorites	Open Bookmark File
Refresh	Reload
Back	Back
Forward	Forward
Stop	Stop
Microsoft	AOL Time Warner

Table 4.1: Microsoft Internet Explorer terms and their Netscape Navigator equivalents

Searching with Yahoo!

Yahoo! (*http://www.yahoo.com/*) is one of the oldest and most valuable Web searching tools. Dozens of workers at Yahoo! visit thousands of Web sites every day and place them in a hierarchical index, providing descriptions and even reviews of the sites they list. Yahoo! can and does often reject a site from its index if it doesn't believe the site to be a valuable or unique resource. (This doesn't necessarily mean *useful:* Yahoo! lists over thirty sites devoted to "munchies" such as the Bacon Worship Page and the Gallery of Regrettable Foods, which reprints horrible cookbooks from the 1930s to the 1950s, including recipes such as the mouth-watering "Beet Pie Casserole.")

Yahoo! doesn't claim to be as comprehensive as a site such as the Open Directory, but this often means the results you do find on Yahoo! are more relevant than those you find elsewhere. One word of caution: Yahoo! has become more commercialized over the years, and occasionally it may point you in the direction of a paid sponsor rather than toward legitimate academic resources.

Other subject directory indexes

Many of the search engines listed below, including Google and AltaVista, now include subject directory options as well (Google's subject directory is based on the Open Directory). Here are some additional, more academically oriented subject directories.

Librarian's Index to the Internet
http://www.lii.org/
This comprehensive site offers reviews of sites listed as well as a very clean organizational structure.

TIP

Advertising on the Web. Many Web directories and search engines are supported by advertising. Recently, advertisers have begun to get more aggressive in order to attract your attention. Ads may appear in **pop-up windows** above your browser window or even **pop-under windows** *behind* your main browser window. To close these ads, just click in the `close window` box in the upper right corner of the window (or the upper left, for Macintosh users).

WWW Virtual Library
http://www.vlib.org
This index is divided into hundreds of categories. Each category is managed by a specialist, so categories are variable in quality, depending on the particular specialist.

The Argus Clearinghouse
http://www.clearinghouse.net/

Searching with Web search engines

Instead of relying on humans to catalog a select (if still very large) list of sites, search engines (often called **robots**) try to automate the process and provide a way of searching the entire Web.

Use search engines when you need to perform a thorough search of the Web's resources. Search engines use computers to index the Web, so they are not limited to the sites human indexers locate. The AltaVista search engine indexes over 100 million Web sites. By typing `Virginia Woolf`, for example, you can find every site in the index that includes either of those words anywhere in its text. Of course, using "Virginia Woolf" as keywords will generate thousands of hits, from bookstores to academic sites to genealogy pages. You'll need to select a few more keywords to narrow your search.

One word of caution regarding searching with most commercial Internet search engines: because they are for-profit enterprises, they constantly seek new ways to profit from their position on the Web. One obvious way they do this is through advertising. It's easy to avoid banner ads if you're not interested, but other ads may not be as obvious. At this writing, for example, Google allows some advertising clients to pay to have their listing appear above the list of search results when you search using a term they specify. Be aware of these and other sorts of commercial messages as you work—remember, your job is to find the best sources for your project, not those that have paid the most to get noticed.

Searching with Google

Perhaps the most ambitious robot search engine, Google (*http://www.google.com/*) attempts to catalog the entire Web by periodically visiting every known site and adding the site's text and images to its database. When you type in a keyword,

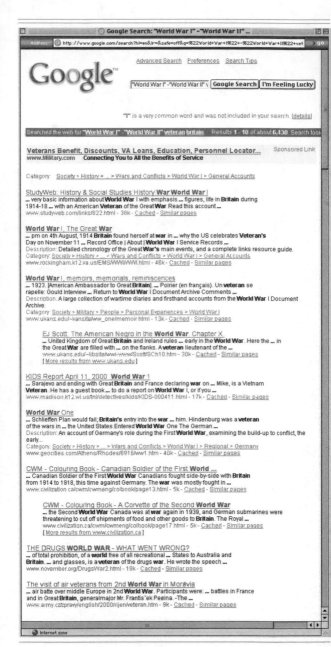

Figure 4.4: A refined search on Google

Advanced searching

Boolean searching

Depending on what you're searching for, basic searches in search engines like Google may not be precise enough to locate the most relevant sources. This is especially true when the keywords you need to use have many different applications. For example, Camilla Gonzales was researching copyright issues regarding the popular MP3 music format. However, she was frustrated when her initial searches returned only entertainment sites—some of the most popular sites on the Web. She next turned to AltaVista's Advanced Search feature (accessed by clicking the Advanced Search button on the AltaVista home page, at *http://www.av.com*). Camilla was then able to refine her search to locate sources concerned with the legal aspects of MP3s rather than entertainment sites. Figure 4.5 shows the result of her search. To narrow her results to the most useful sites, Camilla used **Boolean** operators.

Unlike its regular search function, AltaVista's Advanced Search feature allows the use of powerful Boolean operators. Employing these commands allows you to narrow a search and to bring back a smaller number of **hits**. Hits are simply listings of Web pages containing the search terms you specify. Here are some of the basic Boolean commands—as it turns out, the same commands you use for the various library databases (such as the MLA online index).

Entering	Searches for
world war I	all sites containing the terms *world, war,* and *I*
world AND war	only sites containing both the terms *world* and *war* (note that *AND* is usually necessary only when combining Boolean operators)
world OR war	either *world* or *war*
"world war I" NOT "world war II"	only sites containing the phrase *World War I* but not the phrase *World War II*
pizza*	occurrences of the root within other words: pizzas, pizzacatto, etc. (a **fuzzy search** of *pizza*)

into Yahoo!'s yellow pages—you could end up with hundreds of listings. Take care, too—these sites often point you to fee-based "detective" services you probably don't need.

In academic research, you may be interested in finding a faculty member at a college or university. In this case, it may be easier to go directly to that institution's home page and look for a Search function. How do you find the institution's URL? Do a Yahoo! search.

Searching with other services

There are literally hundreds of other search services out there. Rather than give a lengthy description of each one, we simply provide a selection of their URLs with a brief note or two on the most popular.

Search engines (robots)

Lycos
http://www.lycos.com/
Easy to use, comprehensive. Offers several different rankings of results: popularity, match with search terms, and news sources.

Ask Jeeves
http://www.ask.com/
Surprisingly useful. Designed for beginners, it offers quick answers to many common questions, such as "How do I apply for a passport?" It also displays the results of searches using several different search engines.

Mamma
http://www.mamma.com/
A "meta" search engine; Mamma combines the results of searching all the major search engines into one centralized listing.

HotBot
http://hotbot.lycos.com/
This site, favored by many professionals, offers extensive advanced search features.

Advanced browsing techniques

Search engines aren't the only way to locate information on the Web. Many times, you can get better results by exploiting the structure of a URL. URLs have several different components, and each component can lead you to a different place. Consider the URL for Microsoft's Department of Justice Timeline:

http://www.microsoft.com/presspass/doj/timeline.asp

The directory path consists of narrower and narrower subject divisions within the domain *microsoft.com*. If you want to find out additional press information about Microsoft, you could go to a search engine like Lycos and run an additional search, or you could simply delete the text *doj/timeline.asp* from the location box in your browser, and press Enter. That would take you to an index of the *presspass* directory, which contains many more links to Microsoft corporate information intended for the press.

You can often speed up your browsing by taking advantage of the fact that large institutions usually have easily remembered domain names. For example, you could perform a Yahoo! search to look for Harvard University's Web site, or you could make an educated guess: just type http://www.harvard.edu in your browser's location box. In fact, both Navigator and Explorer will accept partial URLs—just www.harvard.edu works fine. If you're looking for a corporate site, these browsers will even guess the server name and domain type correctly. Typing just microsoft will bring up *http://www.microsoft.com/*.

Other research sites

Using search engines alone won't direct you to some of the most valuable sites on the Web. Internet search engines generally index only Web sites—not the information contained in databases located on the Web. In addition to online magazines, most major newspapers, news magazines, and television news networks have huge, searchable Web sites that allow you to find an immense array of documents on news events. Articles, photos, and other documents from these sites may not be indexed by the major search engines, so the only way to locate these documents is to go directly to the source.

Online magazines

The Web has spawned an entirely new sort of publication: the online magazine or **e-zine**. These publications func-

Chapter 5

Managing Web Site Information

As your research progresses, you'll begin to access a tremendous amount of material. It's temptingly easy to download everything about a particular topic. Before long, you'll end up with a collection of printouts and files that makes no more sense than the vague ideas you had when you began your project. In order for your research to be effective, you need a plan for managing the information you find.

When you start a project, you'll want to skim a few on-line sources to get a sense of the broad context of your chosen research topic. As you work, make a note of the sources that you think will be useful later when you begin to learn more about your topic. You can quickly evaluate a source's usefulness by using your browser's Find command to look for a few key terms that you know are important.

Later, as you focus and narrow your topic, you will want to go back and read these sources more carefully and follow links within them to new research materials. It's essential to set up a system that will make it easy for you to find these materials again when you need them.

Building a document management system

As you locate sources for your research, you need to be able to do two things: access the information you need later, when you need it, and document your sources correctly

image (Macintosh) or clicking the right-hand mouse button (Windows).

Downloading text files is especially useful if there is a limit to the number of Internet-connected computers at your institution. You can take these files and read them on any computer, freeing up the Internet-connected computer for research by other students. Also, since Web sites can be instantaneously changed by their creators, you'll need to preserve your source in its original form to document it for your research. It's a good idea to save the complete text of every online document you use in your research.

The second method is to print out the documents you need. Since traditional research has always relied on print sources, this can give you a sense of comfort and security as you work. But remember that whether or not a document is printed is no sure measure of reliability. Always evaluate each source you use in terms of the guidelines given in Chapter 1.

Downloading helper applications

Some Web sites require **helper applications** in order for you to use the diverse media they offer. Most commonly, you may need a helper application to view video or hear audio files, or to view specialized Web sites incorporating animation or audio. In many cases, the site itself will provide a link to a site that allows you to download the helper application free of charge. For example, to hear Parker Posey reading from the F. Scott Fitzgerald story "Benediction," at *http://www.salon.com/audio/fiction/2001/04/25/fitzgerald/index_np.html*, you need the RealAudio helper application. To download it, you would click on the RealAudio icon, which links you to the RealAudio site at *http://www.real.com/player/index.html*, and then follow the instructions posted at that site.

Generally, files you download will be **compressed**, meaning they are in a special format which must first be uncompressed with yet another helper application before they can be used. For Windows, most files can be uncompressed with WinZip, available at *http://www.winzip.com*. Macintosh files are generally compressed with Stuffit, available at *http://www.aladdinsys.com/*.

Once you've downloaded a helper application, your browser will look for helper applications in a special folder on your hard drive, usually called Plug-ins. For a complete list of plug-ins compatible with Netscape Navigator, visit *http://www.netscape.com/plugins/*.

File Transfer Protocol (FTP)

File Transfer Protocol (**FTP**) is a basic means by which files—including text files, graphics, even applications themselves—are downloaded from and uploaded to central sites by users working at their desktop computers. Transferring files can be a difficult process (though made easier by client programs). Some of the issues you will need to be concerned with are: knowing the address of a site that contains the materials you want, negotiating the directory structure on that site, choosing the right settings for downloading the files, and uncompressing those files to produce the resources you desire. For assistance in using FTP, consult any published guidelines your school's computer support personnel provide for help with FTP and ask your help desk for further assistance as required.

the same subject heading. The "news" at a typical Usenet newsgroup is a mixture of multimedia, personal postings, carefully crafted articles, and conventional newsfeeds. The groups not only distribute these topic-centered materials, but also fulfill an important social function by providing spaces where individuals can meet and engage in discussion.

- **Newsfeeds** represent the most familiar form of news-group information. Groups based on newsfeeds collect traditional news from wire services like the Associated Press and Reuters. Usually found under the large CATEGORY or **Clari** newsgroups, these groups can be extremely useful for basic research, providing instant access to a wide variety of current resources. Check with your instructor about the availability of the Clari newsfeeds at your institution.
- **Moderated groups** operate on the premise that messages posted to the group should be filtered through a moderator; therefore, not every message sent to a moderated list will be posted. Because irrelevant or uninformed posts will be rejected, postings to a moderated list are often well argued and can offer good insight into a research topic.
- **Unmoderated groups** are open to anyone, so messages display varying levels of formality (ranging between scholarly articles and "chat") and often prompt heated debate.

As you use newsgroups, keep in mind that it is often difficult to determine if a message posted on a newsgroup is reliable. For example, a recent message on a stock-market newsgroup recommending the stock of Franklin Mutual Funds turned out to be written by the son of the company president—not exactly an unbiased source.

Web-based discussion

Newsgroups have proved so successful that thousands of Web sites now offer similar features. There are even Web sites that allow you to create your own Web-based discussion forum for free. Most major Web sites such as the *New York Times,* CNN, and Salon now offer some sort of online discussion. The advantage of Web-based discussion is that you don't need to connect to a news server to use it: you can participate using any Web browser with a basic Web connection. However, these sites don't match Usenet's incredibly broad array of newsgroups on nearly every conceivable topic.

Some Web-based discussion sites

Topica
http://www.topica.com
Free hosting service allows you to create your own Web-based discussion forum.

Writer's BBS
http://www.writersbbs.com/forums/
Popular discussion site for writers.

Plastic
http://www.plastic.com/
Dave's favorite discussion site; fast and furious discussion on current events, politics, humor, and more.

How to use newsgroups

Most World Wide Web browsers (see Chapter 4) now incorporate newsreading interfaces that coordinate the reading and composition of newsgroup posts. To point your browser to a newsgroup, type `news:` followed by the name of the newsgroup in your browser's `Location` box. For example, to connect to the newsgroup *alt.activism* you would type `news:alt.activism`. Note: This only works if your institution or Internet service provider offers news hosting.

Finding newsgroups on your topic

Many search engines on the Web allow you to search newsgroups. The most complete index of newsgroups is found at *http://groups.google.com/* (see Figure 6.1 for an example of a Google Groups search). In fact, if you can't connect to Usenet using a news host, you can still find Usenet archives and even post messages using Google's powerful search engine. First Google displays a list of relevant groups, then a selection of archived newsgroup posts that include your search terms. You can view any of these posts, the entire thread to which the post was submitted, or read the newsgroup's entire archive.

Get accustomed to the idea of browsing newsgroups as a means of gathering materials for your research papers and

two other broad categories of messages discussed above: postings from newsfeeds and messages from the "serious," more analytical discussion groups (which often make use of detailed research).

What is significant about Usenet is that most groups make little distinction among all these various types of messages. When you read a magazine, for instance, you may notice that less "authoritative" material such as a letter to the editor is separated from the featured articles. Furthermore, you won't be able to see the many articles that were not selected for publication by the editors. In contrast, when you enter a thread of discussion in a newsgroup, you are instantly surrounded by a number of divergent voices and opinions, all pulling against one another in a variety of ways. If you read through this information with a critical eye, you might actually come to a fuller sense of the complexity of an issue than you might reach after reading isolated printed sources.

Figure 6.2: A newsgroup thread discussing Microsoft founder Bill Gates

Chapter 7

Publishing Your Own Documents on the World Wide Web

It has never been easier to publish your documents on the World Wide Web. Now almost all major word processors allow you to save documents as **HTML** files. HTML, or Hypertext Markup Language, is a special file format that allows your document to be viewed using any Web browser. You need only know a little about HTML in order to share your ideas with nearly a billion Web users worldwide.

One of the things that makes HTML so powerful is that as soon as you've produced your poem, essay, slide show, guidebook, or whatever, it's instantly available to anyone in the world with access to the World Wide Web. The immense size of the Web's audience is also probably the most important thing to keep in mind as you create your Web site. Your audience is the global community of users of the Web, so your Web document should be easy to use for that audience—not the much more limited audience consisting of your classmates and instructor. Put yourself in the shoes of someone who hasn't taken your class, read the books you have, or even used the same kind of computer you're using. Your Web site should be accessible to them, as well as to your local audience.

So while creating a Web page no longer requires any specialized computing skills, creating a *usable* Web site still requires a great deal of planning. As we see it, there are six fundamental components of creating a good Web site. Most industry insiders believe it's much more difficult to find

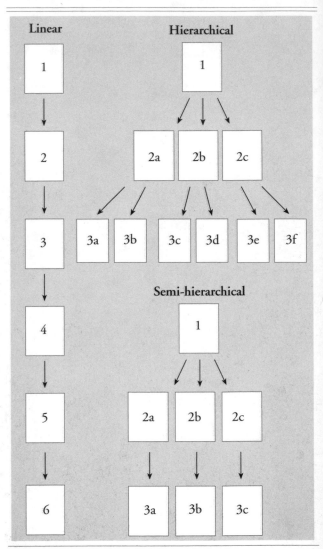

Figure 7.1: Common Web site organizational structures

Presenting information on the Web

The Web allows you to present information in the form of text, still images, sound, video, and animation. Text can be in tables, paragraphs, or even words flying across the screen. Images can be photos, charts, and graphs designed for ornamentation or information. As you consider how to present information, remember that each method has advantages and limitations. Some of these are summarized in Table 7.1. The table is arranged according to increasing memory requirements. It's also important to note that each medium requires specialized software to produce. Though text and image-editing software is relatively abundant, software for animation, audio, and video can be quite expensive.

The media you choose will, of course, depend on your topic. If your Web site analyzes the songs of various birds, for example, then audio will be an essential component. However, if it considers only the poetry of Mary Wroth, then text will likely be the most important medium for your site.

Since text is the "cheapest" in terms of computer memory and time it takes to create, most Web sites contain a lot of text. But if the purpose of a site is to display a collection of photos or original artwork, for example, a lot of text may simply get in the way of the message you're trying to convey. Whatever medium you choose for your Web site, make sure you've made an informed decision.

Type	Advantages	Limitations
Text (TXT)	Uses least memory. Easily printed and saved.	In a graphics-oriented environment, some visitors may lose interest.
Images (GIF, JPEG)	Uses moderate memory. Stable on many different types of computers.	Can be overused. Can take a lot of time to prepare.
Animation (GIF)	Uses moderate memory. Useful when well done.	Can be annoying. Usually in poor taste.
Audio (WAV, AU, MP3)	Only way to present certain types of data.	Uses substantial memory. Can be very annoying. No Internet-wide standard for file format.
Video (AVI, MOV, MPG)	Only way to present certain types of data.	Uses most memory. No Internet-wide standard for file format. Very slow on almost any platform.

Table 7.1:   Advantages and limitations of different information types

Authoring your site

Once you've made the important decisions about what information you will present on your site and how it will be presented, the next step in the process is authoring. **Authoring** is an awkward word, but it is probably the most descriptive term for the process of creating the content material that will be presented on a Web site. Authoring is roughly analogous to writing the manuscript for a book, the script for a play, or taking the photos for a public exhibition. As a content author, you create or obtain from other sources all of the information that will be presented on your site.

Clearly, many different approaches to Web authoring have been successful; however, all successful site authors carefully consider the experience of the visitor as they create content. What might your potential visitor be looking for? What is the clearest, easiest, and most efficient way to give it to them? What information will visitors bring with them? Are there any existing Web sites that provide background information that might be useful to your visitors? What tone and style will be most useful and appealing for your visitors—formal? casual? irreverent?

Content authoring clearly requires proficiency in whatever medium you're producing: writing for text, artistic ability for images, musical ability for sounds. It also requires varying degrees of computer skill, depending on the medium. While writing is an art form that may take years to master, the only technical skill you need to produce text for a Web site is the ability to operate a word processor. In addition to artistic talent, creating images for the Web requires the mastery of one or more **image editors**. An image editor is a computer program designed to create and modify images. The most common image editor for Web applications is Adobe Photoshop. However, almost every program that can create an image can save it in a Web-compatible format. Ultimately, you'll need to create a **GIF** or a **JPEG** image, so make sure whatever image editor you use supports one or preferably both formats. If you're planning to use photos on your Web site, you'll either need access to a **scanner** to convert each photo into a computer file, or you'll need to use a commercial film processor that offers **Photo CD** service.

Guidelines for writing on the Web

Writing on the Web is different from any other form of writing. While printed documents almost universally have a clear beginning, middle, and end, Web sites are accessed in a variety of sequences and contexts, even framed by other sites. Visitors to your site can and often do easily skip on to the relevant portion of your site—or to another site, if they don't find what they're looking for at yours. Keep to the following guidelines unless you have a good reason:

- Since users may enter your site on any page, make sure each page can stand on its own. Help your readers by offering a link to a site map or home page for your site.
- Write in simple, direct sentences that get right to the point.
- Speak directly to your readers: address them as "you," rather than "all of you" or "he or she." Remember, your audience may be thousands of people, but each one of them is generally visiting your site alone with his or her computer.
- Keep paragraphs short—reading long paragraphs on-screen can be tiring.
- Break up your writing with heads and subheads.
- Try to limit each page on your site to no more than one or two screens of information.
- Work Internet links into the context of your writing. Remember that the user doesn't need to see the entire URL of the site you link to—just enough information to identify the site.

Guidelines for creating images on the Web

While it's beyond the scope of this text to discuss the technical aspects of image creation, we can offer a few pointers:

- Keep images as small as possible. Most users have small monitors: 800 by 600 **pixels** is most common, and many monitors offer only 640 by 480. That means your images should probably be no more than 400 pixels wide.
- Use as few colors as possible. The more colors, the more memory your image uses.
- Include only relevant images. Since images take time to download, make sure they are relevant to your discussion.
- On the other hand, don't skimp on images. Users will quickly tire of page after page of text.

TIP

ETHICS: **Using borrowed material.** Make sure you have permission to use borrowed images, words, or other media (see Chapter 8). Remember, copyrighted materials cannot be placed on the Web without permission. If you can't get permission to use a graphic that's already on the Web, you can always include a link to the existing Web site.

Designing your site

Once you've created the content that will appear on your site, you're ready to design the site itself. Perhaps the easiest way to do this is simply to format the text and images you've prepared in your word processor. First create your home page: what will visitors see when they arrive at your site? A table of contents? introductory text? a tone-setting photo? Where will visitors click to get to the main content pages of your site? Will each page include navigational links users can click on to access the main parts of your site, or will visitors be forced to visit each page in sequence? What will your headings look like? Where on each page will images appear? Now is the time to decide on the details of how your site will unfold to visitors.

Once you've made these critical decisions, you're ready to take the final step before actually posting your site on the Web: converting your site into HTML files and image files that can be read by any browser.

Creating a Web page using a word processor

How do you create a Web page? There are three common methods: **exporting** files from your word processor, coding in HTML (see page 80), and using a **Web authoring system** (see page 79). The rest of this section will focus on using a word processor to export Web pages. Since Microsoft Word is the most widely used word processor, our examples will come from Word. However, other word processors, such as Word Perfect, offer similar features.

You'll need to create each Web page on your site separately. Simply format the text and images the way you'd like them to appear online, then select the `Save as Web Page` command from the `File` menu. Type a file name, click on `Save`, and you're all set! You can now open your Web browser, select `Open File` from the `File` menu, and view your first Web page.

Adding basic structure and links

You now know how to make a passable Web page using your word processor. However, your page probably still has a few flaws. It probably still sports a basic, but dull, white background. Most importantly, it likely doesn't contain any links to the rest of the Web, or even to other pages on your site.

Figure 7.2 shows a Web page that has remedied these flaws. The dark background was created in Word by selecting `Background` from the `Format` menu. Links to other pages on the site were also added (see page 74 for more on links). What you can't see in the figure is that the file name has also been changed to *index.html*. This is the standard file name for home pages on most file servers. The benefit of using *index.html* as your file name is that you don't have to

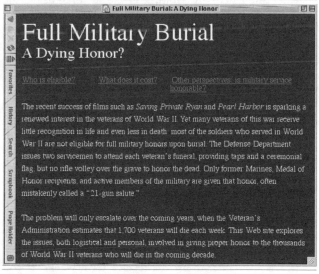

Figure 7.2: **A Web page created using Microsoft Word. This page offers basic formatting and links.**

─── TIP ───

ETIQUETTE: **Linking to other Web sites.** Links give the Web tremendous power because they allow users instant access to other relevant resources. When you link your site to another, as a courtesy you should let the author of that site know you're linking. Make sure you give credit to the authors of sites you link to—don't make it appear as if someone else's work is actually your own. If you display these common courtesies when you create your site, you may be rewarded as well: others will link to your site, and your work will become part of a truly worldwide community.

type it in the location box to point your browser to the file. Just type the domain name and any subdirectories, and your browser will automatically open *index.html*. Note that many campuses now use Windows servers; with this type of server you need to title your home page *default.htm*.

Links

One of the most powerful features of HTML is the ease with which documents from all over the world can be linked together. In Microsoft Word, you create links using the Hyperlink command on the Insert menu. When you create a link, you need to specify two things: the clickable hot text users will see, and the URL of the Web page you link to. Type the URL in the Link To box, and type the text your users will see in the Display box. Click OK.

Relative vs. absolute URLs

When linking to an outside Web site, you always need to use the complete URL (the **absolute URL**), beginning with http://. However, when linking to a file on your own site, you should use the local or **relative URL**. This is a partial URL that takes advantage of the fact that your browser already "knows" the URL of the current Web page. The simplest relative URL is just the name of the file. If you keep all the HTML files on your site in the same directory, you just type the file name in the Link To box; there is no need to type the entire URL.

In fact, it's better to use the relative URL whenever you can; this allows you to keep a complete working copy of your site on your personal computer. In this way, you can test all your links locally before you post your site to the World Wide Web. If you used absolute URLs when building your site, then clicking on the links would take you to the Web, rather than looking for the file you just created on your computer. It would be impossible to test your site before it became available to the entire Internet community.

You can also use relative URLs to link to files in different directories. To link to a file in a subdirectory of the directory you're in, use the following syntax:

```
subdirectoryname/file.html
```

Once you're in a subdirectory, getting back to your site's main directory without resorting to absolute URLs requires another bit of syntax. The notation `../` means "the directory containing the current directory" and can be used to go "backward" in the current directory tree. Thus, if your file is in a subdirectory and you'd like to link back to the main page in the directory containing it, use this syntax:

```
../index.html
```

Because keeping track of relative references can be difficult, many professional Web designers keep all their files in the same directory even if the total number of files exceeds one or two *hundred*. At some point, however, you'll simply have to subdivide—and you'll need to become a relative URL expert. You'd be surprised how handy this skill really is!

Images

In Figure 7.3 we've added a photo to our Web page. The photo was taken using a digital camera and uploaded to the computer using the software and connecting cable that came with the camera. You can also take a photo with a standard camera and scan it in using a scanner (available at many copy stores and college and university computer labs). Or, for a small additional fee, many photo shops will place all your photos on a CD-ROM, which you can then use to place your photos on your Web site.

Once your photo is saved in electronic form, you add it to your Web page using the `Picture--From File` command on the `Insert` menu. When you save your file as a Web page, Word will automatically save the image in the proper format for the Web.

Testing your Web page

As you build your Web page in Microsoft Word, it's easy to check your page to see how it will look on the Web. Just select the `Web Page Preview` command from the `File` menu. Word will automatically save your file and open it in your browser so you can see what it looks like as you work.

The most important difference between a Web page and a Word document is that Web pages always expand to fill the available space, whereas in Word you can set margins to control the width of your document. This difference can be very aggravating for a Web page designer, but remember that visitors to your site may have smaller or larger monitors than you, so it's important for the Web page to resize itself as users resize windows on their computers.

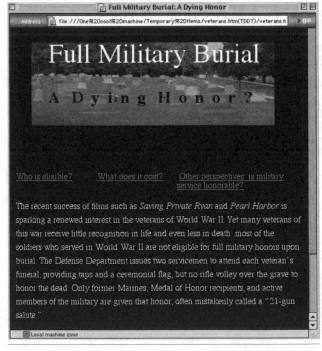

Figure 7.3: A complete HTML Web page, with an image added to enhance the message.

Posting your site to the Web

After you've constructed your site to work perfectly on your local computer, it's time to post it to your institution's Web server. Up until now, you've been the only person with access to your site. Posting your site on the server means that everyone in the world with access to the Web can see your site.

What the server does

Serving files involves two major activities: (1) overseeing the behind-the-scenes operations of the Web server, including setting up form and imagemap routines, and running software that provides the proper protocol for sharing files on the Web; and (2) managing directory structures and files that reside on the Web server. Organizing your files and uploading them to a server may require some time and energy. Whatever your level of technological knowledge, we recommend that you coordinate with your Web administrators as you work through the various tasks involved in serving your files.

Usually your computer services center or some other institutional entity will be responsible for the operations of the Web server, so you will probably not be involved in the first of these two activities (if you do need information about the server-side operations of the Web, see *http://Web66.coled.umn.edu/Cookbook/*). Some institutions will provide students with individual accounts for Web building, but in many cases, the instructor will be responsible for managing files for the entire class.

If your institution does not offer space for hosting Web sites, you can still post your site using a free service such as Geocities (*http://geocities.yahoo.com/*). These services often offer free online tutorials and site-building tools. However, it is generally preferable to use your institution's server for academic sites: not only do you benefit by associating your site with the name and reputation of your institution but your institution also benefits through the opportunity to show off its students' accomplishments. Also, the "free" service of Geocities does come with a price: Geocities will place advertising on your site, which may diminish the serious message you are trying to convey.

Uploading files

There are two main ways to upload your files to your server. If your computer is connected directly to your campus network (for example, a Windows NT network), you may be able to copy your files directly to the server the same way you do locally. Otherwise, you'll probably be using FTP (your institution's Information Technology Services department should be able to help you with this process). No matter how you upload your files, you need to be sure that the final organization of the directories and files that you load to the server mirrors the structure of the files on your computer. If your Web page includes images, Word will automatically save them in a separate folder, and this entire folder must be placed on your site in order for it to work. Additionally, when loading files, send HTML documents and any text files as ASCII text or text only and other media as binary or raw data. Make sure that file names remain unaltered during the uploading process. Finally, after you have placed files on the server, you should check the links with a browser to ensure that nothing has gone wrong.

Publicizing your site

Once you've posted your site, you want people to visit it, right? Otherwise, you might as well have left it on your local computer. Fortunately, there are many free and easy options for publicizing your site on the Internet. The simplest is to post a brief message describing your site (including its URL, of course) on relevant newsgroups (see Chapter 6) and listservs (see Chapter 2).

Next, you may want to try to get your site indexed on the major Web search engines and indexes. Most search engines have an "Add URL" feature that allows you to type your site's URL and a brief description that will appear when your site is listed in someone's search. In addition, you should specify the keywords you'd like your site to be listed under in your page's actual HTML file. You do this by selecting the Properties button from the File menu. Click on the Summary tab and type your keywords in the Keywords box.

Select these words carefully—these are the words that describe how someone might locate your site. Search engines will use these keywords as a way of indexing your site. Think about the words you would use if you were trying to locate a site like yours. You may even want to include common misspellings of your most important keywords.

Building Web pages using authoring systems

Microsoft Word does a good job creating simple Web pages, but since Word wasn't designed specifically to create Web sites, it does have a number of limitations. It's difficult to use Word to create a page that looks truly "professional." Word doesn't offer the kind of precision control needed to create sites that really shine, and it often generates unpredictable results.

For a more polished Web site, you need to use a tool specifically designed for the Web: a Web authoring system. There are dozens of these tools available, but we've divided them into three types: freeware, consumer products, and professional products.

Freeware authoring systems

The most widely used free authoring system is Netscape's Composer, which comes free with its Communicator suite of Web products. Composer produces cleaner, simpler code than Microsoft Word, which many users see as an advantage. However, it doesn't offer the image creation features of Word; you'll need a separate editor to create your images.

Many free Web hosting services, such as Geocities, allow you to create a Web page free using their online tools. These services can be convenient because they eliminate the often troublesome step of posting your site, but they are also often slow and cumbersome, particularly if you have a slow Internet connection.

Consumer authoring systems

Consumer authoring systems such as Microsoft FrontPage offer a substantial leap up in quality from freeware. Usually priced around $100, these systems come with an extensive library of predesigned sites, giving your site a more finished look without much effort on your part. Or you can use the system's tools to create a handsome site on your own. Either way, your site will have a polished look that would be difficult to create in Microsoft Word. Be warned, though: if you use a "canned" site design from one of these systems, your site might look good, but it will also look the same as hundreds—perhaps thousands—of other Web sites.

Professional authoring systems

For the ultimate in control, use a professional Web design system such as Macromedia Dreamweaver or Adobe GoLive. This professional software can cost over $300, so it's definitely not for beginners. This is the software professionals use to create high-traffic Web sites like Salon.com and Hotbot.com. Here are some of the more important features among the thousands these systems offer:

- Instantly see how your page will look as you create it. For example, you could move an image around on the page to determine where it would look best, or experiment with different color schemes to see which you like best.
- Calculate download times to see how long it will take the typical user to view your page.
- Automate the posting of your site to the Web.
- Interactively manage your entire Web site. For example, you could open several pages on your site simultaneously and easily interlink them.
- Make global changes to your site without repeating them on each page. For example, if you want to change the background image on each page, some authoring systems allow you to specify that this change will be implemented throughout your site.
- Seamlessly integrate your site with advanced features such as animated graphics, Javascript, and Shockwave presentations.

Whatever authoring system you select, remember that the main goal of your site is to convey information to your users; sometimes complicated graphics and animation simply get in the way of your message. It's better to say something important in restrained black and white than to say nothing at all in glaring pink and gold animated neon lights.

A guide to HTML commands

Whether you create your site using Microsoft Word or Adobe GoLive, the software is simply creating an HTML file for you. Many Web authors prefer to create the HTML themselves, rather than letting the program do it for them.

Dave created sites in raw HTML for years before finally switching to Dreamweaver about a year ago. But it still pays to have a basic understanding of HTML, so we continue to offer this guide to the basic HTML commands.

Headings

```
<H1> . . . </H1>    Largest heading
<H2> . . . </H2>
<H3> . . . </H3>
<H4> . . . </H4>
<H5> . . . </H5>
<H6> . . . </H6>    Smallest heading
```

Font styles

```
<B> . . . </B>                  Bold-face text
<I> . . . </I>                  Italicized text
<U> . . . </U>                  Underlined text
<TT> . . . </TT>                Typewriter font
<STRIKE> . . . </STRIKE>        Strike-through text
<SUP> . . . </SUP>              Superscript text
<SUB> . . . </SUB>              Subscript text
<BIG> . . . </BIG>              Large font
<SMALL> . . . </SMALL>          Small font
<CENTER> . . . </CENTER>        Centered material
```

Lists and menus

Definition list

```
<DL>
<DT>E-mail
<DD>The basic form
   of Internet com-
   munication.
<DT>Emote
<DD>Virtually rep-
   resents an ac-
   tion during
   real-time conver-
   sations on IRCs
   and MOOs.
</DL>
```

E-mail
   The basic form of Internet communication.
Emote
   Virtually represents an action during real-time conversations on IRCs and MOOs.

Unnumbered list

```
<UL>
<LI>Milk
<LI>Bread
</UL>
```

- Milk
- Bread

Numbered list

```
<OL>
<LI>Milk
<LI>Bread
</OL>
```

1. Milk
2. Bread

Menu list

```
Heading
<MENU>
<LI>Milk
<LI>Bread
</MENU>
```

Heading
Milk
Bread

Links

The most common is the link to a document or file:

```
<A HREF="URL/filename"> . . . </A>
```

You can also make a link to a target within a document. Begin by placing a target anchor in the desired spot in the document.

```
<A NAME="target name">
```

Next, make a link to the target by using the # sign and specifying the target name in the link information.

```
<A HREF="#target name"> . . . </A>
```

You can also link to a sound, graphic, or video file by specifying the proper file name in the link information.

	Links to:
`<A HREF="URL/filename.gif">...</A>`	GIF image
`<A HREF="URL/filename.jpg">...</A>`	JPEG image
`<A HREF="URL/filename.mpg">...</A>`	MPEG movie
`<A HREF="URL/filename.mov">...</A>`	Quicktime movie
`<A HREF="URL/filename.au">...</A>`	Sound file
`<A HREF="URL/filename.wav">...</A>`	Sound file

Inline images

Inline images are graphics that are incorporated into the layout of a Web page. To place an inline image in a document, select the point in the document where the image should appear and use the appropriate command:

```
<IMG ALIGN=bottom SRC="imagefilename.gif">
<IMG ALIGN=middle SRC="imagefilename.gif">
<IMG ALIGN=top SRC="imagefilename.gif">
<IMG ALIGN=left SRC="imagefilename.gif">
<IMG ALIGN=right SRC="imagefilename.gif">
```

HTML, Head, and Body tags

Your entire Web page needs to be structured as follows, using the HTML, Head, and Body tags:

```
<HTML>
<HEAD>
All Head tags go here
</HEAD>
<BODY>
The main tags and text for your Web page go here
</BODY>
</HTML>
```

Background attributes

The background attribute allows the user to specify an image file to use as a background for the Web page. This attribute is applied to the body element. For example, at the beginning of the body section of a Web page, the element `<BODY BACKGROUND="imagename.gif">` tiles the window background with the designated GIF image. When the background attribute is utilized, the end tag to the body section is still simply `</BODY>`.

Colors

Colors can be given to a number of page elements. You can specify the most basic colors by just typing their names: "White", "Red", "Green", etc. In HTML, strict colors are designated by six-character codes. Because of the complexity of these codes, you might refer to one of the many Web sites that provides the codes for the 216 **Web-safe colors** that display correctly on both Macintosh and Windows platforms (for example, *http://webtemplates.com/colors/*). Colors are specified by using a hexadecimal value for each component of the color: red, green, and blue. Colors are usually applied as attributes to the <BODY> element and should be specified in the opening tag. If one of the following attributes is used, they should all be specified in order to avoid color conflicts: if a visitor has set the Web browser to display text in the same color you gave to your background, this would make the page unreadable.

`<BODY BGCOLOR="#rrggbb">`	Sets the background color for the page as a whole
`<BODY TEXT="#rrggbb">`	Sets the text color for the page as a whole
`<BODY LINK="#rrggbb">`	Sets the unvisited link color for the page as a whole
`<BODY VLINK="#rrggbb">`	Sets the visited link color for the page as a whole
`<BODY ALINK="#rrggbb">`	Sets the activated link color for the page as a whole

All these attributes should be specified in a single <BODY> tag, like so:

```
<BODY BGCOLOR="#FFFFFF" TEXT="#000000"
LINK="#FF0000" VLINK="#00FF00" ALINK="#00FF00">
```

Colors may also be applied to selected text within the body of a Web page. The element <FONT COLOR="#rrggbb"> . . . </FONT> will set the color of the text between the tags to the designated shade.

Tables

HTML tables are contained within <TABLE> . . . </TABLE> tags. The fundamental elements of an HTML table are <CAPTION>, which defines a caption for the table, and <TR>, which defines a table row. Each row in turn contains cells, either for a header, defined by <TH>, or for data, defined by <TD>. (Although in this example we are using only numerical data, text and even graphic files can be entered in a data cell as well.) Each cell should be closed with the appropriate ending tag, either </TH> or </TD>.

The caption may be aligned to the top, bottom, left, or right of the table by adding an ALIGN attribute to the <CAPTION> tag. By default, a table is flush with the left margin, but it can be centered by placing the entire table script within <CENTER> . . . </CENTER> tags. Additionally, a BORDER attribute may be added to the <TABLE> tag, which indicates that the table should be drawn with a border around it and between each of the table's cells. Adding a value (in number of pixels) sets the outer border of the table to the specified width.

To combine all these features, you can create a table using the following script:

```
<TABLE>
<CAPTION ALIGN="bottom">Academy Award Winning
African American Actors</Caption>
<TR><TH>Actor</TH><TH>Movie</TH>
<TH>Year</TH></TR>
<TR><TD>Whoopi Goldberg</TD><TD><I>Ghost</I>
</TD><TD>1991</TD></TR>
<TR><TD>Cuba Gooding Jr.</TD><TD><I>Jerry
Maguire</I></TD><TD>1997</TD></TR>
<TR><TD>Louis Gosset Jr.</TD><TD><I>An Officer
and a Gentleman</I></TD><TD>1983</TD></TR>
<TR><TD>Hattie McDaniel</TD><TD><I>Gone with the
Wind</I></TD><TD>1940</TD></TR>
<TR><TD>Sidney Poitier</TD><TD><I>Lilies of the
Field</I></TD><TD>1964</TD></TR>
<TR><TD>Denzel Washington</TD><TD><I>Glory</I>
</TD><TD>1990</TD></TR>
</TABLE>
```

The resulting table would be displayed as:

Actor	Movie	Year
Whoopi Goldberg	*Ghost*	1991
Cuba Gooding Jr.	*Jerry Maguire*	1997
Louis Gosset Jr.	*An Officer and a Gentleman*	1983
Hattie McDaniel	*Gone with the Wind*	1940
Sidney Poitier	*Lilies of the Field*	1964
Denzel Washington	*Glory*	1990

Academy Award Winning African American Actors

You can also experiment with adding the CELLPADDING= and CELLSPACING= attributes to the <TABLE> element, which dictate (in number of pixels) the amount of space surrounding the contents of cells and the width of the borders between cells, respectively. With their more advanced features, HTML tables can provide not simply a way to present data clearly but also a strategy for Web page design itself.

We can take our simple table above to the next level by using more detailed and specific commands. Note that this level of precision requires much more code for what some would consider to be only an incremental improvement.

```
<BODY BGCOLOR="WHITE">
<TABLE CELLPADDING="0" CELLSPACING="0"
WIDTH="350">
<CAPTION ALIGN="bottom" WIDTH="350"><FONT
COLOR="Blue">Academy Award Winning African
American Actors</FONT></CAPTION>
<TR>
   <TD COLSPAN="3" WIDTH="350"><HR></TD>
</TR>
<TR>
   <TD HEIGHT="16" WIDTH="125"
   ALIGN="Left"><FONT
   COLOR="Red"><B>Actor</B></FONT></TD>
   <TD HEIGHT="16" WIDTH="175"
   ALIGN="Left"><FONT
   COLOR="Red"><B>Movie</B></FONT></TD>
   <TD HEIGHT="16" WIDTH="50" ALIGN="Left"><FONT
   COLOR="Red"><B>Year</B></FONT></TD>
</TR>
<TR>
   <TD COLSPAN="3" WIDTH="350"><HR></TD>
</TR>
<TR>
   <TD HEIGHT="16" WIDTH="125"
   ALIGN="Left">Whoopi Goldberg</TD>
   <TD HEIGHT="16" WIDTH="175"
   ALIGN="Left"><I>Ghost</I></TD>
   <TD HEIGHT="16" WIDTH="50"
   ALIGN="Left">1991</TD>
</TR>
<TR>
   <TD HEIGHT="16" WIDTH="125" ALIGN="Left">Cuba
   Gooding Jr.</TD>
   <TD HEIGHT="16" WIDTH="175"
   ALIGN="Left"><I>Jerry Maguire</I></TD>
   <TD HEIGHT="16" WIDTH="50"
   ALIGN="Left">1997</TD>
</TR>
```

```
<TR>
   <TD HEIGHT="16" WIDTH="125"
   ALIGN="Left">Louis Gosset Jr.</TD>
   <TD HEIGHT="16" WIDTH="175"
   ALIGN="Left"><I>An Officer and a
   Gentleman</I></TD>
   <TD HEIGHT="16" WIDTH="50"
   ALIGN="Left">1983</TD>
</TR>
<TR>
   <TD HEIGHT="16" WIDTH="125"
   ALIGN="Left">Hattie McDaniel</TD>
   <TD HEIGHT="16" WIDTH="175"
   ALIGN="Left"><I>Gone with the Wind</I></TD>
   <TD HEIGHT="16" WIDTH="50"
   ALIGN="Left">1940</TD>
</TR>
<TR>
   <TD HEIGHT="16" WIDTH="125"
   ALIGN="Left">Sidney Poitier</TD>
   <TD HEIGHT="16" WIDTH="175"
   ALIGN="Left"><I>Lilies of the Field</I></TD>
   <TD HEIGHT="16" WIDTH="50"
   ALIGN="Left">1964</TD>
</TR>
<TR>
   <TD HEIGHT="16" WIDTH="125"
   ALIGN="Left">Denzel Washington</TD><TD
   HEIGHT="16" WIDTH="175"
   ALIGN="Left"><I>Glory</I></TD>
   <TD HEIGHT="16" WIDTH="50"
   ALIGN="Left">1990</TD>
</TR>
<TR>
   <TD COLSPAN="3" WIDTH="350"><HR></TD>
</TR>
</TABLE>
</BODY>
```

This code produces the following table:

Actor	Movie	Year
Whoopi Goldberg	*Ghost*	1991
Cuba Gooding Jr.	*Jerry Maguire*	1997
Louis Gosset Jr.	*An Officer and a Gentleman*	1983
Hattie McDaniel	*Gone with the Wind*	1940
Sidney Poitier	*Lilies of the Field*	1964
Denzel Washington	*Glory*	1990

Academy Award Winning African American Actors

Note that the specification of a width and height for each table cell allows precise control over the positioning of each element in the table. We used the COLSPAN attribute to generate horizontal rules extending all the way across the table.

You can use tables to position graphics and text as precisely as if you were laying them out on paper. For example, you could use a table to place a directory of your site in column form along the left-hand side of the page, and then create a second column for text. Tables are also used to create the effect of "margins," which are otherwise difficult to create in HTML. Simply make a three-column table with a single   (non-breaking space) character in each of the two outside columns, and run your text down the middle.

When you're using tables and other high-level tricks to give your page a particular look, make sure you test them on both Netscape and Microsoft browsers to verify that all visitors to your site have the same experience.

If you're interested in using tables to give very fine control of the look of your entire Web site, visit David Siegel's Creating Killer Web Sites at *http://www.killersites.com/tutorial/index.html*.

Chapter 8

Giving Credit to Your Sources: Copyright Online

There are two reasons you should give proper credit to your sources:

1. You can get in a lot of legal trouble if you don't.
2. You can get in a lot of academic trouble if you don't.

Almost any work you find on the Internet is protected by copyright. The author of a work has the sole power to determine its use and distribution. It is illegal to reproduce this work in almost any form unless the copyright holder gives you permission. This chapter covers the legal issues surrounding using someone else's ideas in your work. Chapter 9 covers the academic issues in giving credit to your sources.

Here are some situations where copyright issues affect your research and writing online:

1. You download a photograph from a commercial, subscription-based Web exhibition and include it in your Art History paper, citing it according to COS guidelines.
2. You want to post your essay on Gwendolyn Brooks's poem "We Real Cool" on the class Web site. In your essay, you quote the entire poem—eight lines, which you typed in by hand from your textbook—taking care to credit the author of the poem.
3. Someone e-mails you a speech by Kurt Vonnegut. You post it to a national Vonnegut listserv, giving proper

credit in MLA form to the speech's author, Kurt Vonnegut, and obtaining permission from the person who e-mailed you the speech.

4. You have collected MP3s of your twenty favorite songs and want to post them to your personal Web page, housed on the campus server. Some of them come from your CDs, while you found others available online.

5. You publish a scathing critique of Stephen King's latest novel in both the print and online versions of your school newspaper, quoting the entire first paragraph and discussing its failings in detail, pointing to specific examples throughout the book and revealing the plot twist at the book's climax. You obtain no permission from the author or the publisher of the book.

When you reproduce a copyrighted work without the permission of the copyright holder, in most cases, you are violating the law. There are two important exceptions to the law, illustrated in examples 1 and 5 above.

Make single copies of copyrighted work for educational use

You may reproduce a copyrighted work for your personal educational use, as in a paper submitted only to your instructor or discussed in class (assuming you give proper credit to the author, as discussed in Chapter 9). This is the "educational use" provision of the law.

Make many copies of copyrighted work or publish on the Web if it meets fair use guidelines

You may also publish extracts from a copyrighted work if you're publishing a critical analysis or review of the work. You may not reproduce the entire work, however, and you must give credit to the original source. While applications of the law vary, as a rule of thumb, never quote more than 300 words or 10 percent of a work, whichever is less. The logic behind this rule is that copyright law protects the copyright holder's right to control sales or distribution of the work. If your use of the work enables people to obtain it from you rather than from the copyright holder, then you are violating copyright law. This is true even if you do not profit from your actions. The positive side of copyright is that as long as your comments are not libelous, the law protects your right to print even extremely negative criticism of copyrighted works without permission. This is the fair use provision of the law, designed to balance the right of free speech with the right to own property.

Find out if a work is copyrighted before you reproduce it

Never assume a work is not copyrighted, even if you see no copyright notice. Copyright law does not require a notice—any original work you produce is protected by copyright laws unless you explicitly give permission to reproduce it. Here are two cases when it is acceptable to reproduce a work that is not your own without obtaining permission (but you must still give credit to your source):

1. The copyright has expired. In the United States, the law is constantly evolving, but you can be fairly certain a work's copyright has expired if the work was published before 1923. In Great Britain and much of the rest of the world, copyrights generally expire fifty years after the death of the author.
2. The author has given a blanket permission to use the work or placed the work in the public domain (except in the case of government documents, this rarely occurs).

Determining whether the copyright has expired may take some research. Make sure you have determined the most recent revision date of the work you're using. For example, Strunk's *The Elements of Style* was first published in 1909; its copyright has expired and you are free to reproduce that version of the text. However, E. B. White's revision of the text remains copyrighted; you cannot reproduce that work without permission.

Some Web sites offer free graphics and sounds that you may download and use on your own Web page. If you use such images, make sure you comply with any terms of usage posted on the originating site.

Many government documents such as the *Congressional Record* are in the public domain. Be careful, however—even the *Congressional Record* may contain copyrighted material quoted from other sources. When in doubt, request permission.

Request permission to reproduce copyrighted work

If you make a document available to the public, you must get permission to reproduce any copyrighted material it contains. Refer to Table 8.1 to determine whether you need to request permission to reproduce copyrighted material in your document.

Locating the copyright holder

To obtain permission to reproduce the work, you must first determine who holds the copyright. If you're quoting from a source on the Web, look for a copyright statement, usually found at the bottom of the Web page. Often an e-mail link will be provided, and you can e-mail the copyright holder directly. Otherwise, you may need to e-mail the Webmaster for the site to find out who to contact.

If the work you want to reprint comes from a book, the copyright statement is generally found on the page following the book's title page. The copyright holder is generally the author or the publisher, but it might be someone else entirely. Make sure the portion of the book you want to reproduce has not been reprinted from some other work. If it has, you'll probably need to locate the original source to find all the information you need. Even if the author holds the copyright for the work, the best course of action is usually to contact the publisher. Try visiting the publisher's Web site and searching for "permissions department." Many publishers now provide electronic links for requesting permissions. For other publications such as newspapers and magazines, follow a similar procedure.

Sending the letter of request

To request permission to reproduce a work, send a polite letter or e-mail explaining how and where you wish to use the work. Explaining that you are a student and that you in-

	Critical Analysis/ Review	Summary or Para- phrase	Complete or Partial Works
Text			
Paper turned in to instructor	A	A	A
Paper posted to class listserv	A	A	E
Posting to national listserv	300/10	E	N
Newsgroup posting	300/10	E	N
Web site	300/10	E	N
Other Media (Images, Audio, Video)			
Paper turned in to instructor	A	A	A
Paper posted to class listserv	A	A	E
Posting to national listserv	N	E	N
Newsgroup posting	N	E	N
Web site	N	E	N

A: Always okay

E: Educational materials only

N: Never okay

300/10: Okay to reproduce 300 words or 10 percent, whichever is less

Table 8.1: Use this table to determine when it is acceptable to reproduce a copyrighted work without requesting permission from the copyright holder. In each case, you must give credit to the creator.

tend to use the work only for educational purposes will go a long way. Often this process takes several weeks and may result in permissions fees, so you probably want to have a backup plan in case you do not receive permission to reproduce the work you want.

After you receive permission to reproduce a copyrighted work, it is essential that you give the rights holders credit as they specify; otherwise you may still be in violation of copyright law. In addition, you must give proper academic credit to your sources as specified in Chapter 9.

Chapter 9

Giving Credit to Your Sources: Documenting Online Sources

Any time you use someone else's words, images, sounds, or ideas in your academic work, you must give them proper academic credit. Even if you simply "forget" to give credit to your sources, you can fail a class or even be expelled from school for **plagiarism**. You should be aware that if your instructors suspect you of cheating, they can use the powerful tools of the Internet to check your work. Simply by entering a suspicious phrase from your essay into a search engine, an instructor can quickly discover if your work is truly your own.

The most important reason to document your sources is to help others learn from your work. Even if your paper is read only by your instructor, you may have found an idea that your instructor wants to follow up on—the result of your instructor's efforts could be a published book, journal article, or Web site with credit given both to you and to the sources you cite in your paper. If you publish your work on the Web, you could be helping thousands of others learn from your work, and by directing them to the sources for your work, you can help them learn even more.

Determine how sources are documented for your type of project

Because research and learning can take many different forms, each discipline has its own rules for how to document sources. For example, scholars in the Humanities are often interested in the actual written words, so the author and page number are given in Modern Language Association (MLA) citations. Social scientists are often more interested in how recently a study was conducted, so the author and date are given in American Psychological Association (APA) citations. Your instructor might specify additional rules or guidelines based on the needs of your class. Be sure to check on your course syllabus or with your instructor to determine the proper method for documenting sources in each class.

Using the Columbia Online Style to document electronic sources

It is beyond the scope of this book to give guidelines for documenting every type of source in every discipline. However, many disciplines have not yet published usable guidelines for citing electronic sources, so here we offer a brief summary of the Columbia Online Style (COS for short). COS was developed by Janice R. Walker and Todd Taylor to address some of the shortcomings of MLA and APA documentation styles. Be sure to get your instructor's permission before you use COS to document sources. For more information about COS, visit the COS Web site at *http://www.columbia.edu/cu/cup/cgos/*, or consult *The Columbia Guide to Online Style* by Janice R. Walker and Todd Taylor (New York: Columbia University Press, 1998).

Documenting sources usually consists of three steps:

1. Collect information about your source.
2. Format the documentation according to COS guidelines.
3. Integrate the source material into your project.

Documentation is easiest if you collect the required information when you locate your source. It may be difficult or even impossible to retrace your steps if you need to get additional information later. The remainder of this chapter will show you how to document online sources using the COS–MLA format. Though we do offer a general APA example, if you need to use COS–Scientific style format, you should visit the COS Web site or consult the printed version of the guide.

Collecting information about your source

COS documentation requires six basic pieces of information about each source you cite:

- Author
- Title of work
- Title of larger work containing the work
- Publication date
- Electronic address
- Date of access

Sometimes not all of this information is given for your source. Make an effort to collect all available documentation information when you first locate the source. To save time later, you may want to go further and format the reference for each source into COS style as soon as you locate it. If your computer has enough memory, keep your word processor and a Web browser open at the same time while you are researching. You can avoid errors if you make a habit of copying and pasting each source's documentation information directly from the source into a text file.

Formatting the documentation according to COS–Humanities guidelines

List each source you use on a separate "Works Cited" page and arrange them alphabetically by author (or title, if no author name is provided). Follow the general format below.

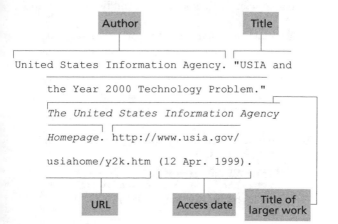

COS Documentation Examples. Though it is important to understand the general format of COS style, it can also be helpful to see how this format is applied to specific examples. When you locate a source, match the type of source you find to the examples below. For example, if you locate a Web site that gives a date for the last time it was updated, then you would format your documentation like example number 2: Web site, revised.

1. Web site

```
Tada, Yuriko. "Intelligible Differences: On
    Deliberate Strategy and the Exploration
    of Possibility in Economic Life."
    Professor Charles F. Sable. 1997.
    http://www.columbia.edu/~cfs11/
    IntelDif.html (12 Apr. 1999).
```

2. Web site, revised

Replace the publication date with the revision date.

```
Martin, Dave. "Honors Requirements." Davidson
    College: Department of Economics. Rev. 26
    Jan. 1999. http://www.davidson.edu/
    academic/economics/honors.html
    (12 Apr. 1999).
```

3. Web site with institutional/group/corporate author

Replace the author name with the publishing institution.

```
American Institute of Indian Studies (AIIS).
    "South Asia Art Archive: Kanchi: Slide
    3373." Center for Electronic Text and
    Image. Rev 7 Apr. 1998. http://www.library
    .upenn.edu/etext/sasia/aiis/architecture/
    kanchi/3373.html (12 Apr. 1999).
```

4. Web site with no author or sponsoring institution

```
"Invasion of the Big Apple." German UFO
    Watch. http://aircooledmind.org/
    alien3.html (12 Apr. 1999).
```

5. Web site maintained by an individual

Use the abbreviation "maint." to indicate an individual who simply collects links or other material but does not significantly contribute to the content on a site.

```
LeMar, Jason, et al., maint. "Indiana
    Academy Science Events." The Indiana
    Academy for Science, Mathematics, and
    Humanities. http://www.bsu.edu/
    teachers/academy/scievents.html
    (12 Apr. 1999).
```

6. Web site—government

For regularly updated sites, give only the access date.

```
United States Information Agency. "USIA and
    the Year 2000 Technology Problem." The
    United States Information Agency
    Homepage. http://www.usia.gov/usiahome/
    y2k.htm (12 Apr. 1999).
```

7. Web site—book available in print and online

Give information on both the printed text and online version when available

```
Shakespeare, William. As You Like It. 1600.
    Ed. Alan Brissenden. Oxford: Oxford UP,
    1994. http://www-tech.mit.edu/
    Shakespeare/Comedy/asyoulikeit/
    asyoulikeit.html (16 Apr. 1999).
```

8. Web site—online article

```
Roulston, Christine. "Separating the
    Inseparable: Female Friendship and Its
    Discontents in Eighteenth-Century France."
    Eighteenth Century Studies. 32:2 (1999).
    http://muse.jhu.edu/journals/
    eighteenth-century_studies/v032/32
    .2roulston.html (14 Apr. 1999).
```

9. Web site—news service/online newspaper article

If no author's name is given, list the name of the news service. Otherwise, cite as an online article.

```
Associated Press. "India's Government
    Resigns." USA Today. http://www.usatoday
    .com/news/world/nwssat01.htm (18 Apr.
    1999).
```

10. Web site—article from an archive

Cite as you would a printed article, but list the name of the archive site ("Archives" in this case) before the URL.

```
Rosenberg, Yuval. "Fox Fights Parkinson's."
    Newsweek. 30 Nov. 1998. "Archives."
    http://newsweek.washingtonpost.com/nw-srw/
    issue/22_98b/tnw/today/nm/nm01we_1.htm
    (16 Apr. 1999).
```

11. Web site with frames

Some Web sites are programmed to divide your browser window into several smaller windows called **frames**. Depending on how the frames have been programmed, the URL displayed in your browser may not correspond to the actual URL of the particular frame you are referencing. Cite as you would an unframed Web page, but list the URL of the main frames page, followed by the instructions for getting to the page you are referencing.

```
Strapex AG. "Industries."  Rev. 27 Oct.
    1996. Strapex. http://www.strapex.com/
    Industries (21 Apr. 1999).
```

12. Web site—image, audio, or video file

You may list the URL of the source file or the Web page on which it appears. If no separate title of the resource is given, list the file name.

```
Aui-Yonah, Yael. "The World of Creation."
    http://www.art.net/TheGallery/vision/
    yael2.htm (16 Apr. 1999).
```

13. Personal e-mail

Do not give the author's e-mail address.

```
Shepard, Mary. "Graduation." Personal e-mail
    (13 Apr. 1999).
```

14. Listserv

Include the address of the list. Do not give the author's
e-mail address.

```
Seabrook, Richard H. C. "Community and
    Progress." cybermind@jefferson.village
    .virginia.edu (22 Jan. 1994).
```

15. Newsgroup

Give the author's name or alias, the subject of the message, posting date, the newsgroup URL, and date of access.

```
ctakim. "Unfair to Call Bill Gates an
    Obnoxious Egotistical Bully." 21 Apr.
    1998. news:alt.conspiracy.microsoft
    (19 Apr. 1999).
```

16. Gopher or FTP site

```
Greenpeace. "Greenpeace Tours North Oil Rigs
    on Brett Spar Anniversary." Greenpeace
    Campaign Archive. 1996. Gopher://gopher
    .greenpeace.org:70/00/campaigns/oceans/
    1996/jun20 (16 Apr. 1999).
```

17. Telnet site

Include any steps necessary to access the relevant information after the Telnet address, separated by a single space.

```
"Experimental Nuclear Reaction Date
    Retrieval Program." National Nuclear Data
    Center. telnet://bnlnd2.dnc.bnl.gov
    (16 Apr. 1999).
```

18. Synchronous communication

Give the name (if known) or alias of the speaker, the type of communication (e.g., personal interview), and the address.

```
Pine_Guest. Personal interview.
    Telnet://world.sensemedia.net 1234
    (12 Dec. 1994).
```

19. Online encyclopedia article

List by author (if available), and give the online service you used to access the article (if not accessed via the World Wide Web).

```
"Roland (de La Platiere), Jeanne-Marie."
    Encyclopedia Britannica Online.
    http://www.eb.com:180/bol/
    topic?eu=85963&sctn=1 (16 Apr. 1999).
```

20. Online dictionary article

List by the word you looked up and give the online service you used to access the article (if not accessed via the World Wide Web).

```
"Slag." WWWebster Dictionary. Merriam-Webster
    Online, 1999. http://www.m-w.com/cgi-bin/
    dictionary (16 Apr. 1999).
```

21. Material from a CD-ROM

List author (if available) and title. Include the version number and copyright date.

```
"Women's Suffrage Multimedia Map." The
    Grolier Multimedia Encyclopedia. Vers.
    7.0.4. Danbury, CT: Grolier, 1995.
```

22. Software

```
Microsoft Word. Vers. 98. Redmond, WA:
    Microsoft, 1998.
```

TIP

ETIQUETTE: **Linking to online sources.** If you publish your project on the Web, format the "Works Cited" section as links (see page 74) to sources available online. Link the in-text reference to the citation and format the URL of the source as a link to the actual resource. As a courtesy, be sure to ask your sources for permission to link to them. Some Web sites give blanket permission to link; in this case it is still appropriate to notify the Webmaster that you have linked to the site so they can alert you if the URL changes.

Integrating the source material into your project

When you begin creating your project, whether it's a research paper, oral presentation, poster, or Web site, you need to make sure you give credit to your sources each time you use information from them. In most cases, this is done with a parenthetical reference to the author and page number. However, since most documents on the Internet don't have "pages" like books or journals, the page number can be omitted, like this:

```
The Grateful Dead didn't mind people taping
their concerts but didn't want to see people
selling the tapes for profit (Barlow).
```

If you work the author's name into the text itself, you don't need a parenthetical reference at all for Internet sources (for print sources, you would always need to add the page number in parentheses).

```
Grateful Dead member John Perry Barlow points
out that the band didn't mind people taping
their concerts as long as they didn't sell the
tapes for a profit.
```

Try to make parenthetical references as inconspicuous as possible—the point is to give your readers an opportunity to refer to your source, not to intrude into the flow of your project.

If the work you cite has no author, substitute the title in quotation marks, or an abbreviated version of the title if the title is long.

Brief guidelines for using COS–Scientific style

The main difference between the COS–Humanities style and the COS–Scientific style is that in most scientific disciplines, scholars place more importance on the date of the work cited, while in the humanities, the actual words written or spoken are seen as more important. "Works Cited" are called "References" in the scientific style, and the date of the work comes immediately after the author name in the reference list.

List all sources you use together on a separate "References" page and arrange them alphabetically by author (or title, if no author name is provided). Follow the general format below. For more specific guidelines, consult *The Columbia Guide to Online Style.*

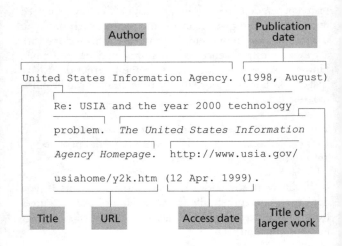

When you integrate the source material into your project, make sure you reference both the author (or title) and date of the work:

```
The Grateful Dead didn't mind people taping
their concerts but didn't want to see people
selling the tapes for profit (Barlow 1998).
```

Chapter 10

A Case Study: Researching Literature on the Internet

Researching literature on the Internet poses some unique challenges. Writing has traditionally required only a pen or pencil and paper, and the literary community has taken time to embrace the publishing and research possibilities of today's high-tech world. Why? Publishing is the primary goal for "serious" poets, dramatists, writers, and critics, but online publication has not been valued as highly or considered as prestigious as print publication. Also, because the literary community understands that copyright law is complex, it has only slowly placed literature and criticism on the Internet.

With those concerns in mind, the Internet provides tremendous resources for literature researchers. These resources tend to be the most comprehensive in two areas—works like Sophocles's plays, Elizabeth Barrett Browning's poetry, or Nathaniel Hawthorne's novels, whose copyrights have expired; and "nontraditional" literature such as cowboy poetry, which has often been excluded from the mainstream press. Extensive biographical information on individual authors is also available electronically. Popular authors or literary movements (like the Beat Writers) may even have several fan pages. Newsgroups and listservs offer up-to-the-minute conversations on current issues in literature and criticism. Finally, the Internet has made libraries worldwide accessible to everyone—provided you allow enough time to request their materials via interlibrary loan. The rest of this chapter will take a step-by-step approach, following a student, Frank Miller, as he completes his research project.

Step 1: Identify your topic

Frank is taking Introduction to Literature and was assigned a major research paper on "an important theme in a work covered in this class." The assignment requires that he draw on at least ten outside sources and analyze the text closely in developing his argument. In the unit on Literature and War, the class read Virgina Woolf's *Mrs. Dalloway*. Because he enjoyed that novel and found the character of a tormented war veteran, Septimus Smith, particularly intriguing, Frank has decided to write his paper about some aspect of Woolf's novel and World War I.

Step 2: Narrow the focus of your topic and begin to formulate your thesis

One good way to find information to help narrow your topic is to browse with a Web subject directory. (For more on Web subject directories, see page 38.) Frank chooses Yahoo! at *http://www.yahoo.com/* and begins to click on directory topics (see Figure 10.1). He clicks on progressively narrower topics: Arts and Humanities, Humanities, Literature, Authors, World War I. But when he gets to the World War I site, he finds a list of writers such as Rupert Brooke and Wilfred Owen, but no Virginia Woolf.

Stumped, he backs up several levels to see where his search may have gone wrong. This time, instead of selecting World War I, he selects Literary Fiction; this sends him to a lengthy list of authors, including Woolf. Happily, he discovers several scholarly web sites devoted to Woolf, including the International Virginia Woolf Society (*http://www .utoronto.ca/IVWS/*). After visiting these sites and reading some commentary, he narrows his topic:

```
Virginia Woolf's Mrs. Dalloway
Insanity and Mrs. Dalloway
World War I veteran Septimus Smith and Mrs.
Dalloway
Treatment of war veterans in postwar Britain
and Mrs. Dalloway
```

As Frank works, he records addresses for the sites he may want to revisit later.

When you're brainstorming for a topic, you could also try looking through the past postings in a newsgroup (see step

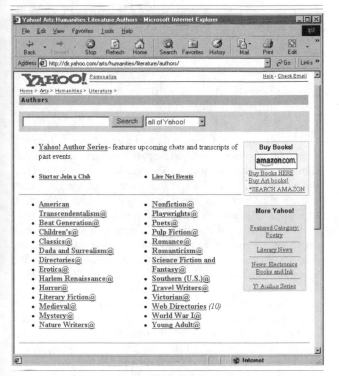

Figure 10.1: The "Authors" subject directory in Yahoo!
*Reproduced with permission of Yahoo! Inc. © 2000 by
Yahoo! Inc. YAHOO! and the YAHOO! logo are
trademarks of Yahoo! Inc.*

4)—it might give you an idea for your paper just by seeing
what other people are talking about. Although he doesn't
find generalized newsgroups talking about Woolf, he does
find a chat group focused on her at *http://www.western
canon.com/* as well as a Virginia Woolf bulletin board on a
Woolf Web site, where he posts a query.

Step 3: Create a research plan

Frank makes a new folder on his computer's hard drive ti-
tled "Virginia Woolf Project." He creates a Works Consulted
document to keep track of the print and electronic sources
that have been helpful thus far and saves it to this folder. He
also makes a new Favorites folder on his computer's Web
browser for the topic (for more on Favorites, see page 36).

Frank has decided to keep track of his sources in a text file on his computer. For more on managing Web research, see Chapter 5.

Step 4: Investigate and join newsgroups and listservs

Newsgroups (see Chapter 6) and listservs (see Chapter 2) allow you to observe and participate in ongoing discussions about your research topic. It's a good idea to observe and join these groups early in the research process so you get a sense of how they can help you. Frank goes to List Universe at *http://www.list-universe.com/* and searches for relevant public listservs using the keyword "Virginia Woolf." His first search on Virginia Woolf found no matches. He tries again, this time narrowing the search to discussion list sites, and again gets no matches. He tries instead with "World War I Literature," but again gets no match.

At this point, Frank decides to try another search, this one using Topica, a site devoted to newsletters and discussion groups. He gets no results with searches for "Virginia Woolf" and "World War I." However, after browsing around on the site, he uses the Topica subject headings to do progressively narrower searches, from Humanities to History to Periods to Twentieth Century, and finally, decides to join a discussion group (modslist) that focuses on modernism and modernists (see Figure 10.2). Although this group will probably not talk about the specific character, Septimus Smith, that his paper will focus on, Frank may find some good general discussion about World War I and art. However, he does find a private scholarly listserv (the VWOOLF list), which is housed at Ohio State, through the International Virginia Woolf Society Web page. He checks on both lists periodically as his work proceeds.

Once you have an idea for a topic, you can post your own message to get feedback about your ideas. When posting to bulletin boards, listservs, or newsgroups, remember to compose a posting that shows you've put some serious thought into the topic. The message, "I am writing a paper on *Mrs. Dalloway;* can anyone help me?" will probably get only sarcastic responses if it gets any responses at all.

A carefully composed request that perks the interest of others in the group is much more likely to generate useful and interesting responses. While group members will probably pass by a subject line like "*Mrs. Dalloway* paper," they will be intrigued by a more specific one, such as "A question about shell-shock and Septimus in *Mrs. Dalloway.*"

Step 5: Follow up on links uncovered in steps 2–4

Don't forget to keep notes on the sites you visit while you're narrowing and refining your topic; you never know when they might become useful. After Frank decides to focus on Woolf's depiction of Septimus as it relates to the real psychological and social treatment of British World War I veterans, he looks back on his notes and revisits the World War I pages from his initial Yahoo! search. These lead to some magazine stories written by and about wounded soldiers during the war (*http://www.hcu.ox.ac.uk/jtap/hydra/*).

Figure 10.2: The twentieth-century history page in the
Topica directory of mailing lists

Step 6: Gather additional material and conduct searches using Web search engines

Once you've done some preliminary research, it's time to dig deeper into your topic. The best way to find highly specialized information on the Web is to use Web search engines (see pages 41–48). Frank decides to use Lycos at *http://lycos.com/* to perform a phrase search for "Virginia Woolf." By placing the name in quotation marks, he limits his search to sites that include the two names together. This search yields almost 32,000 hits. He decides to focus on the novel itself by using the + operator:

```
+"Virginia Woolf" +"Mrs. Dalloway"
```

This yields over 2,600 hits—greatly reduced, but still obviously too much information. Frank notices that the results contain many advertisements for and reviews of the recent film version of the novel. He modifies his search again to exclude references to the film by using the – operator:

```
+"Virginia Woolf" +"Mrs. Dalloway" –film
```

This strategy helps, reducing the number of hits to 170. Frank will still need to weed through the listings, which range from publisher's advertisements to relevant discussions. The keywords that will enable you to narrow your search efficiently will vary according to author and topic.

Step 7: Evaluate your sources

This step is ongoing at every stage in the research process. When Frank looked at the Web site with a link to World War I–era stories about veterans and decided that the information provided legitimate evidence about contemporary attitudes toward mental illness, he was evaluating the source. This is particularly important when doing research on the Internet, where anyone can post or present information on any subject. It is not monitored or regulated for authenticity by anyone except whoever's viewing it.

More information on evaluating Internet sources can be found in Chapter 1.

Step 8: Look for electronic texts of works on the Web

While most copyrighted books and journals are not freely available on the Web, famous works whose copyrights have expired can be found in abundance. In the United States, all copyrights for works published before 1922 have expired, so if you're writing about a work published before then, you may very likely find the complete text on the Web. In Great Britain, copyrights expire fifty years after the death of the author, so you may even find some published after 1922 on the Web (for example, many works of D. H. Lawrence can be found at the Bibliomania Web site, *http://www.biblio mania.com/Fiction/dhl/*).

Frank finds that some works of Virginia Woolf are available on the Web, and some are even searchable. Although *Mrs. Dalloway* is not available online, Frank does find out from the Virginia Woolf Web site (*http://orlando.jp.org*) that there is a CD-ROM with search features as well as a microfiche concordance—available in some libraries—for each of Woolf's major novels. If you have a searchable text, be sure to look for alternate spellings or synonyms as well.

While counting instances of key words does not substitute for a close analysis of the text itself, searching Web text can alert you to key passages you may not have noticed otherwise. Some Web search engines even allow commands like "before" and "near," which can further limit your search. Below are several sites that offer searchable text of literary works.

The American Classical League—University of Michigan
http://www.tlg.uci.edu/~tlg/index/resources.html

IPL Online Texts Collection
http://www.ipl.org/reading/books/

Electronic Text Center—University of Virginia
http://etext.lib.virginia.edu/english.html

The Internet Classics Archive—Massachusetts Institute of Technology
http://classics.mit.edu/

Isle of Lesbos: Lesbian Poetry
http://www.sappho.com/poetry/

The On-Line Books Page—University of Pennsylvania
http://digital.library.upenn.edu/books/

Step 9: Search for additional sources in the library

For most research projects, you should always supplement the information you find on the Internet with resources from the traditional libraries. After narrowing his topic with help from the Internet (step 2), Frank returns to his campus library, where he had previously been overwhelmed by the massive number of critical articles and many books about Woolf's work. Now he is able to use keyword searching in the Modern Language Association database to locate books and articles that pertain specifically to his topic area. In this search, he finds several relevant articles published recently, as well as a book about World War I in literature that has a chapter on *Mrs. Dalloway.* As his library does not have the book or a couple of the articles he needs, he orders these materials online through interlibrary loan. He copies two other articles to review as he continues his search for electronic sources.

You can also use the Internet to search the online catalog of your school library and other libraries for books. Most online library catalogs are similar to each other, but it is helpful to read the search directions for each one to ensure that you are getting the best responses. An easy way to search many different libraries is to use the Library of Congress WWW/Z39.50 Gateway at *http://lcweb.loc.gov/z3950/gateway.html#other*. You can also search indexes, such as Carl UnCover (*http://www.carl.org/*). This particular index provides access to journal articles, which can be faxed to you for a fee.

Step 10: Write your paper

Once you've collected enough information, it's time to begin composing. Frank starts by going through the information he's collected and writing a thesis and an outline. As he begins composing his paper, occasionally he has trouble motivating himself to write. Once again, the Web can help. Many sites are dedicated to student writing; here are some of the best:

The Online Writery
http://www.missouri.edu/~writery/

Purdue Online Writing Lab
http://owl.english.purdue.edu/

University of Texas Undergraduate Writing Center
http://uwc.fac.utexas.edu/resource/

Paradigm Online Writing Assistant
http://www.powa.org/

Frank visits the Purdue site and finds a handout, "Writing about Literature: Some Helpful Things to Know," that helps him clarify his thesis and link his quotations and secondary sources effectively into his argument. As Frank writes, he is careful to document all sources he uses according to COS–Humanities style. (For more on COS style, see Chapter 9.)

Additional sites for researching literature on the Web

Author sites

Playwrights on the Web: International Playwrights & Their Online Plays
http://www.stageplays.com/writers.htm

An Index of Poets in Representative Poetry On-line
http://www.library.utoronto.ca/utel/rp/intro.html

Geoffrey Chaucer (ca.1343–1400)
http://www.luminarium.org/medlit/chaucer.htm

Edmund Spenser Home Page—Cambridge University
http://www.english.cam.ac.uk/spenser/main.htm

Criticism on the Web

Elizabethan Review
http://www.elizreview.com/

Ophelia
http://www.stg.brown.edu/projects/hypertext/landow/victorian/gender/ophelia.html

Sewanee Review
http://cloud9.sewanee.edu/sreview/Home.html

MFS
http://www.sla.purdue.edu/academic/engl/mfs/

Postmodernism, Deconstructionism, Criticism, and
Literary Theory Campfire messsage board
http://killdevilhill.com/postmodernchat/wwwboard.html

Voice of the Shuttle: Literary Theory Page
http://vos.ucsb.edu/shuttle/theory.html

Poetry Daily, a new poem every day
http://www.poems.com/

Zuzu's Petals Literary Links: General Reference Tools
http://www.zuzu.com/

VoS English Literature: English Literature Page
http://vos.ucsb.edu/shuttle/english.html

Chapter 11

A Case Study: Researching Science on the Internet

Researching scientific topics on the Internet may seem fairly simple. Search for almost any topic, from coral bleaching to viral transfer, and you are guaranteed to come up with thousands of hits. Many of these will be highly reputable Web sites sponsored by governmental and professional associations with stellar credentials. You can get electronic texts of articles from professional journals. You can watch medical operations online. In fact, the problem may seem to be one of choosing between too many good sources.

However, researching scientific topics online also poses some challenges. Scientific research relies heavily on scrutiny by other scientists (a process formally known as *peer* or *juried review*) to test the accuracy of research methods and the validity of results. Sometimes studies are published electronically prior to undergoing a rigorous review. A further complication is that the information you can find electronically may be too general. Some of it, in fact, will be inaccurate, presented by "doctors" who want to sell you new cures and remedies or by well-meaning amateurs (such as parents describing a child's medical condition). The rest of this chapter will take a step-by-step approach, following a student, Paula Richardson, as she completes her research project.

Step 1: Identify your topic

Paula is taking a writing-intensive introductory biology course, Science in the News, that focuses on scientific writing for the general public. Students are required to write a major research paper that "explains a complex health issue to a general audience." The assignment requires that she draw on a variety of outside sources, include illustrations as relevant, and provide her audience with a list of additional resources.

Initially stumped for a topic, Paula decides to investigate heart murmurs. Her cousin has one, as does a close friend. While her cousin has restricted physical activity because of her murmur, Paula's friend played varsity soccer in high school. Figuring out how and why the condition can affect people so differently, Paula decides, would be an interesting topic for her article.

Step 2: Narrow the focus of your topic and begin to formulate your thesis

One good way to find information to help narrow your topic is to browse with a Web subject directory. (For more on Web subject directories, see page 38.) Paula chooses the Open Directory Project at *http://www.dmoz.org/* and begins to click on directory topics (see Figure 11.1). She picks progressively more narrow headings: Health, Conditions and Diseases, Cardiovascular Disorders, Congenital Anomalies. At this point, however, the possible links seem rather general and make no mention of heart murmurs.

Paula backs up two levels to Conditions and Diseases, where she realizes that she'd overlooked an alphabetical site index. She clicks on M and finds Murmurs amid a long list of conditions. This link leads her to an impressive list of sources on the subject. After investigating a number of sites and calling home to learn her cousin's specific diagnosis, she decides to narrow her focus to explore the causes of and treatments for murmurs caused by flawed aortic valves. As Paula works, she records addresses for the sites she may want to revisit later.

When you're brainstorming for a topic, you could also try looking through the past postings in a newsgroup (see step 4)—it might give you an idea for your paper just by seeing

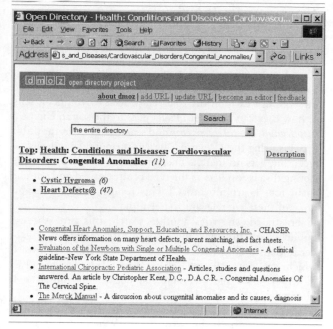

Figure 11.1: The "Congenital Anomalies" subdirectory in Open Directory

what other people are talking about. Paula finds a message board at *http://www.parentsplace.com/*, where parents talk about their experiences in raising children with a variety of medical conditions.

Step 3: Create a research plan

Paula makes a new folder on her computer's hard drive entitled "Heart Murmurs." She creates a Works Consulted document to keep track of the print and electronic sources that have been helpful thus far and saves it to this folder. She also makes a new Favorites folder on her computer's Web browser for the topic (for more on Favorites, see page 36). Paula has decided to keep track of her sources in a text file on her computer. For more on managing Web research, see Chapter 5.

Step 4: Investigate and join newsgroups and listservs

Newsgroups (see Chapter 6) and listservs (see Chapter 2) allow you to observe and participate in ongoing discussions about your research topic. It's a good idea to observe and join these groups early in the research process so you get a sense of how they can help you. Paula goes to the search engine at *http://www.list-universe.com* and searches for relevant public listservs using the keywords "heart murmurs" and "heart defects" but gets no match. Then she narrows her search by selecting discussion lists as the type of site desired and searches again for "heart murmurs." This results in four hits, but none of these are relevant to her topic.

Frustrated, she tries another search, this time through Publicly Accessible Mailing Lists, at *http://paml.net/*. Again, her initial search generates a list of over 20 listservs, most of which are not relevant to her topic (see Figure 11.2). However, a couple are, and she decides to subscribe to Hearttalk-l.

Once you have a topic idea, you can post your own message to get feedback about your ideas. When posting to bulletin boards, listservs, or newsgroups, remember to compose a posting that shows you've put some serious thought into the topic. The message: "I am writing a paper on heart murmurs; can anyone help me?" will probably get only sarcastic responses if it gets any responses at all. A carefully composed request is much more likely to generate useful and interesting responses. While group members may pass by a subject line like "Heart murmur paper," they will be interested by a more specific one, such as "A question about treatments for flawed aortic valves."

Step 5: Follow up on links uncovered in steps 2–4

Don't forget to keep notes on the sites you visit while you're narrowing and refining your topic; you never know when they might become useful. After Paula decides to focus on her cousin's type of heart murmurs, she looks back on her notes and remembers that she'd found some message board postings from parents discussing their concerns about their children at *http://www.parentsplace.com/*. She is intrigued by the idea of writing an article about this type of heart defect for a parenting magazine. So, Paula rereads those postings more carefully and notes any resources mentioned. She also goes to the message board and leaves a query about the challenges of being a parent of a child with an aortic valve defect.

Step 6: Gather additional material and conduct searches using Web search engines

Once you've done some preliminary research, it's time to dig deeper into your topic. The best way to find highly specialized information on the Web is to use Web search engines (see pages 41–48). Paula decides to use Google at *http://www.google.com/* to perform a phrase search for aortic valve defects. This search yields over 6,600 hits. She decides to focus more specifically on treatments for the condition:

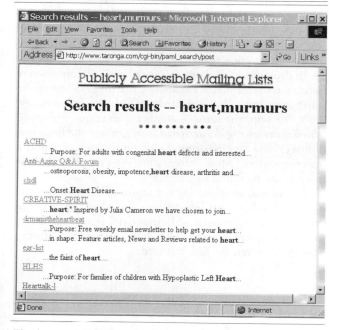

Figure 11.2:   Results of a search for "heart murmurs" at Publicly Accessible Mailing Lists

```
treatments for aortic valve defects
```

This yields over 980 hits—greatly reduced, but still obviously too much information. Paula notices that the results contain many general sites that focus on a wide range of heart defects. She modifies her search again to exclude references to other kinds of defects by using the – operator:

```
treatments for aortic valve defects —mitral
-septal
```

This strategy helps, reducing the number of hits to 295. Paula will still need to weed through the listings to find the most reputable and specific sites for her project. The keywords that will enable you to narrow your search efficiently will vary according to author and topic.

Step 7: Evaluate your sources

This step is ongoing at every stage in the research process. This is particularly important when doing research on the Internet, where anyone can post or present information on any subject. It is not monitored or regulated for authenticity by anyone except whoever's viewing it.

In Paula's case, the large volume of health information resources available makes researching her topic seem easy, but she has to assess the credentials of Web site sponsors carefully. For help, she turns to another Web resource (***http://hi tiweb.mitretek.org/docs/criteria.html***), where she finds published criteria for evaluating the appropriateness or quality of these resources. More information on evaluating Internet sources can be found in Chapter 1.

In addition to evaluating her sources, Paula also is careful to record full citation information, including date accessed, for any sites she may use. Electronic documents are usually not permanently archived. Therefore, any reference must acknowledge when the link was made.

Step 8: Look for electronic texts of works on the Web

However limited your library holdings may be in terms of periodic publications, the Internet expands that library exponentially, as full texts of many scientific articles are available online. Some journals are fully available online, while other sites function as clearinghouses for all kinds of scientific research, such as:

Elsevier's Science Direct
http://www.sciencedirect.com/

Proceedings of the National Academy of Sciences (USA)
http://www.pnas.org/
Archives 1990–present (1960–1996 in JSTOR).

Science Online, which contains *Science* magazine
http://www.sciencemag.org/

JSTOR
http://www.jstor.org/
Please note that JSTOR is designed to be several years behind the current issues.

Be warned: even journals that claim to reproduce full texts of articles sometimes do not. For example, Paula finds what seems to be a full-text article through JSTOR; it looks so helpful that she locates the original in her library. Then she realizes that the electronic version had omitted both the credentials of authors and the accompanying graphs and charts, considerably lessening its value as a source.

Step 9: Search for additional sources in the library

For most research projects, you should always supplement the information you find on the Internet with resources from traditional libraries. You can also use the Internet to search the online catalog of your school library and other libraries for books. Most online library catalogs are similar to each other, but it is helpful to read the search directions for each one to ensure that you are getting the best responses. An easy way to search many different libraries is to use the Library of Congress WWW/Z39.50 Gateway at *http://lcweb.loc.gov/z3950/gateway.html#other.*
You can also search indexes, such as Carl UnCover (*http://www.carl.org/*), Academic Universe (*http://web.lexis-nexis.com/universe/*), General Science Abstracts, or a more specific database in a disciplinary area.

Step 10: Write your paper

Once you've collected enough information, it's time to begin composing. Paula starts by going through the information she's collected and trying to outline it. She realizes that she has two possible arguments she wants to make. Which one will be better for her course? Once again, the Web can help. Many sites are dedicated to student writing; here are some of the best:

The Online Writery
http://www.missouri.edu/~writery/

Purdue Online Writing Lab: Online Writing Lab
http://owl.english.purdue.edu/

University of Texas Undergraduate Writing Center
http://uwc.fac.utexas.edu/resource/

Paradigm Online Writing Assistant
http://www.powa.org/

Paula visits the Purdue site and finds a handout, "Writing a Research Paper: Constructing Effective Thesis Statements and Research Questions," that helps her decide upon a thesis. As Paula writes, she is careful to follow the guidelines for incorporating research that her professor recommended. She finds additional help at Writing Guidelines for Engineering and Science Students (*http://fbox.vt.edu/eng/mech/writing/*). Paula is also careful to document all sources she uses in COS–Scientific style. For more on Columbia Online Style, see Chapter 9.

Additional sites for researching science on the Internet

Biology

BioChemNet
http://biochemlinks.com/bclinks/bclinks.cfm

Neurology
http://www.neuropat.dote.hu/histol.htm

Human Genome Project
http://www.nhgri.nih.gov/HGP/

National Library for the Environment
http://www.cnie.org/nle/

National Center for Biotechnology
http://www.ncbi.nlm.nih.gov/

National Oceanic and Atmospheric Administration's Oceans
http://www.noaa.gov

The Tree of Life
http://phylogeny.arizona.edu/tree/phylogeny.html

Chemistry

Chemdex: Directory of Chemistry
http://www.chemdex.org

Chemistry Web Internet Resources
http://www.ssc.ntu.edu.sg:8000/chemweb/htmlj/

Environmental studies

Best Environmental Directories
http://www.ulb.ac.be/ceese/meta/cds.html

Amazing Environmental Organization Web Directory
http://www.webdirectory.com/

Enviroinfo
http://www.deb.uminho.pt/fontes/enviroinfo

Mathematics

MathSearch
http://www.maths.usyd.edu.au:8000/MathSearch.html

Mathematics Web sites around the world
http://www.math.psu.edu/MathLists/Contents.html

Medicine

Medscape Today
http://www.medscape.com/

MedWebPlus
http://www.medwebplus.com/

National Institutes of Health
http://www.nih.gov/

Physics

Academic Info Physics Resources
http://www.academicinfo.net/physics.html

PhysicsWeb tiptop
http://physicsweb.org/TIPTOP/

Directory of URLs Referenced in the Text

Search engines

AltaVista
http://www.av.com/

Ask Jeeves
http://www.ask.com/

Google
http://www.google.com/

Google newsgroup search
http://groups.google.com/

HotBot
http://hotbot.lycos.com/

List Universe
http://www.list-universe.com/

Lycos
http://www.lycos.com/

Mamma
http://www.mamma.com/

Subject directories

The Argus Clearinghouse
http://www.clearinghouse.net/

Librarian's Index to the Internet
http://www.lii.org/

Open Directory Project
http://www.dmoz.org/

WWW Virtual Library
http://www.vlib.org/

Yahoo!
http://www.yahoo.com/

Web-based mailing lists

Listbot
http://www.listbot.com/

Topica
http://www.topica.com/

Yahoo! Groups
http://groups.yahoo.com/

Web-based discussion sites

Plastic
http://www.plastic.com/

Topica
http://www.topica.com/

Writer's BBS
http://www.writersbbs.com/forums/

125

General research sites

Academic Universe
*http://web.lexis-nexis.com/
universe/*

Boolean Search Tutorial
*http://www.learnthenet.com/
english/html/77advanc.htm*

Carl UnCover
http://www.carl.org/

Columbia Online Style Web site
*http://www.columbia.edu/cu/
cup/cgos/*

Criteria for Assessing the
Quality of Health Information
on the Internet
*http://hitiweb.mitretek.org/docs/
criteria.html*

Encarta
http://encarta.msn.com/

Encyclopedia Britannica
http://www.britannica.com/

Evaluating Web sites and
information
*http://www.namss.org.uk/
evaluate.htm*

Free On-Line Dictionary of
Computing
*http://www.InstantWeb.com/
D/dictionary/*

Library of Congress home page
http://www.loc.gov/

Library of Congress page for
searching different libraries
*http://lcweb.loc.gov/z3950/
gateway.html#other*

Publicly Accessible Mailing Lists
http://paml.net/

Reference for Internet lists
http://tile.net/

Using Cyber-sources Web site
*http://www.devry-phx.edu/
lrnresrc/dowsc/integrty.htm*

Online libraries

Bartleby.com
http://bartleby.com/

Project Gutenburg
http://promo.net/pg/

Questia
http://www.questia.com/

News sites

ABC
http://abcnews.go.com/

CNN
http://cnn.com/

MSNBC
http://msnbc.com/

New York Times
http://www.nytimes.com/

Seattle Times
*http://seattletimes.nwsource
.com/*

Time Magazine
http://time.com/

Washington Post
*http://www.washingtonpost
.com/*

E-zines

Opinion Journal
http://opinionjournal.com/

Salon
http://www.salon.com/

Slate
http://slate.msn.com/

Internet access providers

AT&T
http://download.att.net/partners/

DirecPC
http://www.direcpc.com/

EarthLink
http://www.earthlink.net/

Road Runner
http://www.rr.com/

Helper applications

Directory of plug-ins compatible with Netscape Navigator
http://www.netscape.com/plugins/

Eudora
http://www.eudora.com/

RealAudio site
http://www.real.com/player/index.html

Stuffit
http://www.aladdinsys.com/

WinZip
http://www.winzip.com/

Technical help sites

Creating Killer Web Sites
http://www.killersites.com/tutorial/index.html

Geocities
http://geocities.yahoo.com/

Learn the Net
http://www.learnthenet.com/

Server-side operations of the Web
http://Web66.coled.umn.edu/Cookbook/

Web-safe colors
http://webtemplates.com/colors/

Online text collections

The American Classical League—University of Michigan
http://www.tlg.uci.edu/~tlg/index/resources.html

Edmund Spenser Home Page—Cambridge University
http://www.english.cam.ac.uk/spenser/main.htm

Electronic Text Center—University of Virginia
http://etext.lib.virginia.edu/english.html

Geoffrey Chaucer
http://www.luminarium.org/medlit/chaucer.htm

The Internet Classics Archive—Massachusetts Institute of Technology
http://classics.mit.edu/

IPL Online Texts Collection
http://www.ipl.org/reading/books/

Isle of Lesbos: Lesbian Poetry
http://www.sappho.com/poetry/

The On-Line Books Page—University of Pennsylvania
http://digital.library.upenn.edu/books/

Poetry Daily, a new poem every day
http://www.poems.com/

Science journals online

Elsevier's Science Direct
http://www.sciencedirect.com/

Proceedings of the National Academy of Sciences (USA)
http://www.pnas.org/

Science Online
http://www.sciencemag.org/

JSTOR
http://www.jstor.org/

Authors on the Internet

D. H. Lawrence at the Bibliomania Web site
http://www.bibliomania.com/Fiction/dhl/

An Index of Poets in Representative Poetry On-line
http://www.library.utoronto.ca/utel/rp/intro.html

International Virginia Woolf
Society
http://www.utoronto.ca/IVWS/

Playwrights on the Web:
International Playwrights &
Their Online Plays
*http://www.stageplays.com/
writers.htm*

Virginia Woolf Web site
http://orlando.jp.org/

Biology

BioChemNet
*http://biochemlinks.com/
bclinks/bclinks.cfm*

Human Genome Project
http://www.nhgri.nih.gov/HGP/

National Center for
Biotechnology
http://www.ncbi.nlm.nih.gov/

National Library for the
Environment
http://www.cnie.org/nle/

National Oceanic and
Atmospheric Administration's
Oceans
http://www.noaa.gov/

Neurology
*http://www.neuropat.dote.hu/
histol.htm*

The Tree of Life
*http://phylogeny.arizona.edu/
tree/phylogeny.html*

Chemistry

Chemdex: Directory of
Chemistry
http://www.chemdex.org/

Chemistry Web Internet
Resources
*http://www.ssc.ntu.edu.sg:8000/
chemweb/htmlj/*

Environmental studies

Amazing Environmental
Organization Web Directory
http://www.webdirectory.com/

Best Environmental Directories
*http://www.ulb.ac.be/ceese/meta/
cds.html*

Enviroinfo
*http://www.deb.uminho.pt/
fontes/enviroinfo/*

Literary criticism

Elizabethan Review
http://www.elizreview.com/

MFS
*http://www.sla.purdue.edu/
academic/engl/mfs/*

Ophelia
*http://www.stg.brown.edu/
projects/hypertext/landow/
victorian/gender/ophelia.html*

Postmodernism,
Deconstructionism, Criticism,
and Literary Theory Campfire
messsage board
*http://killdevilhill.com/
postmodernchat/wwwboard
.html*

Sewanee Review
*http://cloud9.sewanee.edu/
sreview/Home.html*

Voice of the Shuttle: Literary
Theory Page
*http://vos.ucsb.edu/shuttle/
theory.html*

VoS English Literature: English
Literature Page
*http://vos.ucsb.edu/shuttle/
english.html*

Western Canon
http://www.westerncanon.com/

Zuzu's Petals Literary Links:
General Reference Tools
http://www.zuzu.com/

Mathematics

MathSearch
*http://www.maths.usyd.edu.au
:8000/MathSearch.html*

Mathematics Web sites around
the world
*http://www.math.psu.edu/
MathLists/Contents.html*

Medicine

Medscape Today
http://www.medscape.com/

MedWebPlus
http://www.medwebplus.com/

National Institutes of Health
http://www.nih.gov/

Physics

Academic Info Physics
Resources
*http://www.academicinfo.net/
physics.html*

PhysicsWeb tiptop
http://physicsweb.org/TIPTOP/

Writing

The Online Writery
*http://www.missouri.edu/
~writery/*

Paradigm Online Writing
Assistant
http://www.powa.org/

Purdue Online Writing Lab
http://owl.english.purdue.edu/

University of Texas
Undergraduate Writing Center
http://uwc.fac.utexas.edu/resource/

Writing Guidelines for
Engineering and Science
Students
*http://fbox.vt.edu/eng/mech/
writing/*

Miscellaneous

Example of Longman textbook
companion site
*http://www.awlonline.com/
lannontech/*

F. Scott Fitzgerald story
"Benediction"
*http://www.salon.com/audio/
fiction/2001/04/25/fitzgerald/
index_np.html*

Harvard University
http://www.harvard.edu/

Joke awards
*http://www.thecorporation
.com/icon/icon.html*

Library of Congress Federal
Credit Union
http://www.lcfcu.org/

Magazine stories by and about
wounded soldiers
*http://www.hcu.ox.ac.uk/jtap/
hydra/*

Microsoft's Department of
Justice Timeline
*http://www.microsoft.com/
presspass/doj/timeline.asp*

MP3.com Web site
http://www.mp3.com/

ParentsPlace.com
http://www.parentsplace.com/

Glossary

@ (the "at" sign) Used to separate the mailbox name from the domain name in e-mail addresses.

absolute URL The complete URL; used to refer to URLs outside of the current domain.

address Specialized URL for sending e-mail, consisting of a mailbox name and the domain name, separated by the @ sign. Also used to refer to any URL.

angle bracket (>) 1. Used to denote a reply quotation in e-mail messages. 2. Used in pairs to surround HTML tags.

application Any type of commercial, shareware, or freeware computer program (usually with a user interface).

ASCII text (pron. *askey*) Also known as "text only" format, the basic, unformatted numbers, letters, and symbols supported by most computer operating systems.

asynchronous Communication or other interaction that takes place with a substantial delay, e.g., e-mail, answering machines.

attachment A file included with an e-mail message.

AU An audio file format commonly found on the World Wide Web.

authoring The process of creating hypermedia content for the World Wide Web.

bit The smallest unit of computer memory. Can have only two values, 1 or 0.

bookmark See *Favorites*.

Boolean Logical search operators that allow a user to refine the scope of keyword searches. The simple Boolean operators are *and*, *or*, and *not*.

browser A program that allows users to view pages on the World Wide Web. The two most popular browsers are Microsoft Internet Explorer and Netscape Navigator.

browsing The process of viewing Web pages with a browser.

byte A unit of computer memory corresponding to eight bits. A byte contains enough information to specify one character.

cable modem A modem that allows you to connect to the Internet using cable TV lines. Cable modems provide nearly instantaneous access to the Internet.

CD-ROM A compact disc used for storing computer files. Many new formats have been introduced recently, including CD-RW, DVD, and CD-R.

chat Any online real-time discussion.

chat room A virtual room on the Internet for conducting real-time discussions.

Clari Newsfeeds from Reuters and the Associated Press in the form of Usenet newsgroups. Institutions must pay a fee in order to subscribe to groups provided by the Clarinet company.

client Software that communicates with a server to provide an easier interface for a user.

Columbia Online Style A method of documenting online sources for academic research, usually in conjunction with MLA or APA style.

Common Gateway Interface (CGI) A program that resides on a server and handles complex information requests. CGIs act as mediators between a source of information on a server and a client. They are most commonly used to process forms in HTML.

compression Manipulation of a file to decrease the amount of memory it uses. Compression can be "lossy" or "lossless," depending on whether data is lost in the process.

dial-up access Connection to the Internet using a modem.

direct subscriber line (DSL or ADSL) A service provided by phone companies that allows high-speed connection to the Internet using regular phone lines.

directory A subdivision in a computer file system (known as a *folder* in some operating systems). Directories can contain files, applications, or other directories.

directory path The complete set of nested directories needed to locate a particular file. In URLs, each directory name is separated by a slash.

discussion list See *listserv.*

domain An element of an Internet or e-mail address specified by an organization or suborganization on the Internet (e.g., *netscape.com, davidson.edu*).

domain type The element of an Internet address that indicates the type of organization hosting the site (e.g., *.edu, .com, .gov*).

DOS See *operating system.*

downloading Retrieving a file, application, or e-mail message from a distant computer over the Internet.

e-mail (electronic mail) A form of Internet communication used to send all types of electronic correspondence to individuals or groups of Internet-connected users around the world.

e-mail address See *address.*

emote To virtually represent an action during real-time conversations.

emoticons Pictures made of text symbols attempting to express emotions in e-mail messages, newsgroup postings, and real-time discussions. The basic Internet emoticon is the *smiley,* a sideways happy face: :-) (turn your head to the left to see it).

export To save a file in a different format; often used for creating Web pages with a word processor.

e-zine A magazine distributed solely by electronic means, usually in the form of a Web site.

FAQ (frequently asked questions) A document that collects and responds to some of the most common questions about a particular aspect of the Internet or about a particular topic, especially in newsgroups and listservs.

Favorites A set of electronic pointers to Internet sites that can be recalled for future reference. Also known as *bookmarks.*

file An electronic document. Files can be in ASCII text, in a format for a particular program, or in a standardized format for sound, graphics, or video (e.g., WAV, GIF, or MPEG).

file name The name of a file, including any extensions such as *.html* or *.gif,* but not including its directory path.

flame A message or posting attacking a message or an individual. A flame usually has a confrontational tone and offers little or no constructive criticism.

form A Web page that allows you to provide information to an online database or an individual via e-mail.

frame An area of a Web page that can display a separate Web page.

freeware Software distributed free of charge.

FTP (File Transfer Protocol) An efficient system for downloading and uploading files on the Internet.

fuzzy search A search for any occurrence of a sequence of characters, regardless of whether they form an entire word.

GIF (Graphical Interchange Format) (pron. *jiff*) A compressed graphics file format frequently used for images on the World Wide Web. GIF files save memory by limiting the number of colors in an image.

Gopher A precursor to the World Wide Web. A good place to find archaic computer programming jokes.

group 1. A list of e-mail addresses a user creates in order to send messages to a group of people with common interests. 2. A newsgroup.

hardware The mechanical portion of a computer system.

helper application Software that works with an Internet application (such as a browser) to add additional features (such as the capability to listen to real-time audio).

hit 1. An item returned from a keyword search. 2. A single visit to a Web site.

history A list of sites recently visited; often automatically maintained by your Web browser.

home page Conventional name given to a central site on the World Wide Web. This name can be used both for the central page of an organization site and for the personal page of an individual within an organization.

host An Internet-connected machine that serves files to other Internet-connected machines.

hot An area in a hypermedia document that is linked to another document. The most common way to link documents on the Web. Hot text is generally colored and underlined to indicate that clicking on it will take the user to another document.

HTML (Hypertext Markup Language) A scripting language used to turn plain text and other elements (such as images) into the integrated pages we see on the Web.

HTTP (Hypertext Transport Protocol) An Internet protocol that allows for the transfer of hypertext files from a Web server to a Web client application.

hypermedia A medium that extends the principles of hypertext to document types other than text.

hypertext A text authoring medium with no predetermined organizational structure, which allows authors to freely link any portion of a document with any other portion or with other documents.

ichat A Web interface for conducting real-time discussions.

image editor A program that allows users to create and edit image files.

imagemap An image that has been "mapped" by HTML commands so that clicking on different portions of it will link the user to different sites or files.

Internet The worldwide network of computers that allows distribution of e-mail, browsing the Web, and countless other ways to access and distribute information.

IP address (Internet Protocol address) The address that is specific to a single computer and identifies it for the purpose of interacting with other computers on the Internet.

IRC (Internet Relay Chat) A system of Internet protocols and programs that allows users to participate on topic-centered, real-time discussion channels.

ISP (Internet service provider) A service that allows individual users to connect to the Internet, for example, via phone or cable TV lines.

Java A programming language that allows computers running on different operating systems to run the same programs. Java functions, typically used for graphics, animation, or complex data management tasks, are actually performed by applications ("applets") which reside on servers rather than individual PCs.

JPEG (Joint Photographic Experts Group) (pron. *JAY-peg*) A graphics file format frequently used for images on the World Wide Web. JPEG files are typically most effective for photographs and offer several different levels of compression, with higher compression resulting in more loss of file resolution.

keyword 1. A word or group of words used in an electronic search to locate documents about a particular topic. 2. A descriptive word or group of words specified by the author or indexer of a document to facilitate electronic searches.

kilobits per second (kbps) A unit for measuring the rate of information transfer. The larger the number, the faster the rate.

kilobyte (K) A unit of computer memory corresponding to 1,024 bytes.

link A hypertext connection between documents, sites, and other media. Note that *link* is commonly used both as a noun to indicate the actual connection between one node and another and as a verb to indicate the process by which this connection is achieved.

Listproc A type of mailing list software. See also *listserv*.

listserv Also known as a *mailing list* or *list*. A program that distributes mail to be sent to a group of addresses.

literal search A search for an exact phrase or grouping of words, usually indicated with quotation marks.

local In the same directory as the current file. In HTML coding, local files can be accessed using relative URLs.

lurk To read a newsgroup or e-mail list for a period of time without posting messages.

Macintosh See *operating system*. See also *platform*.

mail server A server that organizes, stores, and distributes e-mail messages to various users.

mailbox name The specific identification or name given to an e-mail user. In conjunction with the domain name, it makes up the e-mail address using the syntax `mailboxname@domainname`.

mailing list See *listserv.*

Majordomo A type of mailing list software. See also *listserv.*

modem Short for *modulater-demodulater,* a device used to connect computers via a telephone line or other communication link to a server.

moderator Person responsible for determining the relevancy of messages posted to a moderated newsgroup or listserv. A moderator forwards only "appropriate" messages to the group.

MOV/MOOV A video format often used on the World Wide Web.

MP3 A popular format for transmitting audio files over the Internet.

MPEG (pron. *EM-peg*) A video format often used on the World Wide Web.

MU*s (also MUSHs, Tiny MUSHs, MOOs, etc.) Text-based virtual spaces (*Multi User Dungeons* or *Domains*) that allow users to interact in real time with other users or with the textual environment. The different acronyms refer to different programs that perform similar functions.

name search A search for the first and last name of a person. Usually indicated by capitalizing both terms.

netiquette A set of rules for behavior on the Internet, usually dictated by convenience and common sense.

news server Also known as a *news host.* A server that organizes, stores, and distributes newsgroup messages.

newsfeed A message posted to a newsgroup that originates from a wire service or other traditional news source.

newsgroups Topic-centered sites where visitors can exchange articles, messages, or other media. See also *Usenet.*

newsreader A program for accessing and posting to newsgroups.

nickname 1. An address book entry for one or more e-mail addresses. When a user types the nickname, the computer sends that message to each of the addresses in the nickname file. 2. A character name used to log on to IRC channels.

operating system The software that controls the basic operations of the computer. Examples include Mac OS, DOS, Linux, and Unix. These systems are generally incompatible with each other.

page Part of a Web site corresponding to a single HTML file.

PC 1. Also referred to as *IBM compatible,* indicates a computer that runs the DOS operating system (usually with the graphical user interface Windows). 2. Used less often to indicate any personal computer.

Photo CD A type of CD-ROM containing photo images. Also used to refer to the format Photo CD images are saved in.

phrase search See *literal search.*

pixel A single dot, or element, of a picture. Image sizes on the Web are measured in pixels.

plagiarism Intentionally or accidentally presenting someone else's work as one's own. A serious offense—can be grounds for failing a course or expulsion.

platform A computer with a given type of operating system, for example, Macintosh, PC, or Unix.

plug-in See *helper application.*

pop-under window A new window appearing behind your current browser window; often used for commercial purposes.

pop-up window A new window appearing in front of your current browser window; used for either commercial purposes or to add functionality to a Web page.

post 1. To send an electronic message to an e-mail discussion list or newsgroup. Also used as a noun to refer to the message itself. 2. To upload a Web site to a Web server.

protocol The "language" that a client and server use to distinguish various types of Internet media.

readme file Gives information about a piece of software or an Internet forum. Titling a file "readme" almost assures that it will never be read.

real-time discussion Communication or other interaction that occurs almost instantaneously, as in chat rooms, allowing users to communicate in a way that resembles face-to-face conversation. Contrast to e-mail and newsgroup messages, which are asynchronous.

relative URL A partial URL used to specify locations within the current domain.

reply quotation A copy of a message included in the reply to the message. Most mail clients and newsreaders place angle brackets (>) in front of a quotation in order to distinguish it from a new message.

robot See *search engine.*

satellite access A service that allows a high-speed connection to the Internet using satellite signals.

scanner A machine that converts photographs and other physical images into electronic files.

search engine A program usually accessed via a Web site that allows users to perform keyword searches on the Internet (e.g., AltaVista, Infoseek).

search index See *subject directory.*

server 1. Software that provides information to client programs. Clients and servers "talk" to each other to allow the transfer of files and protocols across the Internet. 2. The machine on which a server program is located.

shareware Like *freeware*, software that is made available through the Internet. The authors of shareware ask for a small voluntary fee from users.

signature file Preformatted text attached to the bottom of most e-mail and newsgroup messages which generally contains the author's name, e-mail address, and institutional affiliation (if any). Signature files can also contain carefully constructed ASCII text pictures and favorite quotations.

site A collection of documents on the Internet providing a single set of information to users who access the location.

smiley See *emoticon.*

software A computer program written to perform various tasks, as opposed to *hardware,* which refers to the mechanical parts of a computer system. See also *application.*

spam 1. E-mail sent to large numbers of recipients without their first requesting it. 2. Postings of irrelevant messages to newsgroups or listservs. 3. Any attempt to push unwanted information on Internet users by making use of repetitious computing power. 4. (Rarely used) (*cap.*) A pork-based luncheon meat.

subject directory A directory of services on the Internet organized hierarchically.

Telnet A terminal emulation protocol. With a Telnet client application, such as NCSA Telnet, you can establish a connection to a remote computer.

text only See *ASCII text.*

thread A newsgroup or listserv posting and a series of replies on the same topic, usually with the same subject heading.

tunneling Accessing a site by digging down through various directories or subdirectories.

Unix See *operating system.* See also *platform.*

uploading Placing a file or application on a remote host over the Internet. Often used to put text, sound, graphics, video, and HTML files on a Web server for publication.

URL (Uniform Resource Locator) The address assigned to each document on the Internet. Consists of the protocol, followed by two slashes, the domain name and type, the directory path, and the file name.

Usenet Part of the Internet which facilitates the exchange of messages and discussion. The broad classification of Usenet contains thousands of topic-centered newsgroups organized hierarchically by name.

user name or **user's name** See *mailbox name.*

virus A computer program designed to spread from computer to computer, in a manner analogous to the way a biological virus spreads among living organisms. Most electronic viruses are now transmitted via e-mail attachments. While many viruses are benign, others can cause significant damage by destroying files or disabling programs. Even more troubling is the fact that, unlike natural viruses, computer viruses are created by people. It is our sincere hope that a special place in hell is reserved for virus programmers.

WAV An audio file format.

Web authoring system Software that allows users to create Web pages without using the HTML language.

Web browser See *browser.*

Web-safe colors A set of 216 colors for Web pages that display accurately on all properly equipped platforms.

Web site See *site.*

window A framed area on a computer screen that allows the user to view information without affecting the rest of the screen.

Windows See *operating system.*

workstation An individual computer usually connected to a network but primarily occupied by a single user. Can use one or more of a variety of *operating systems.*

World Wide Web Abbreviated *WWW* or *the Web.* A worldwide system for distributing hypermedia, allowing users to easily navigate between sites and post their own documents.

For more information about computer terms, visit the Free On-Line Dictionary of Computing at *http://www.InstantWeb.com/D/dictionary/.*

Index